2H

1.17.5⁰⁰

Net 2.5⁰

To: EMILY

Fr: STEVE

DEC 2012.

WITH LOVE

D1580363

CHEIRO'S LANGUAGE OF TH

CHEIRO'S
LANGUAGE OF THE HAND

A COMPLETE PRACTICAL WORK ON THE SCIENCES
OF CHEIROGNOMY AND CHEIROMANCY
CONTAINING THE SYSTEM AND
EXPERIENCE OF

CHEIRO

New York

Published by ARCO PUBLISHING COMPANY, Inc.
219 Park Avenue South, New York, N.Y. 10003

27th Edition

33rd Printing

Copyright

All Rights Reserved

Part of this book is Copyright © Arc Books, Inc. 1964

Library of Congress Catalog Card Number 62-16458

Arco Catalog Number 964

DEDICATION

... What do I bring?
Kind Life, 'tis but a little thing,
  A flower I loved in youth;
A flower upon the wayside thrown,
Yet one the lips of truth have known,
  ... And is itself a truth.

CHEIRO.

PREFACE

To believe is to perceive—either by the senses or the soul. This distinction constitutes two classes—the sceptic and the believer, which, though dependent on, may yet be incomprehensible to, each other; but both being necessary to establish the balance of thought, they are forced into existence and become the links and cross-links which make life's endless chain from thought to truth.

In placing the following work before the public, though deeply conscious of my responsibility, I am also conscious of the good that may be derived through such a study. I have therefore endeavoured to write, not for any distinct class, but for all, believing in the ultimate universal acceptance of those natural laws which constitute nature and control mankind, and which are peculiarly exemplified by this study of the hand.

A trifle is concealed immensity—the atom is equal to the whole in the importance of its existence; if, therefore, this study be considered by some too trivial for their attention, I would remind them that many of the greatest truths the world has known, though once considered trivialities, have become sources of infinite power. I would ask of such people nothing more than that they investigate this "atom" for themselves, resting assured that the study will prove its truth, whether examined from the palmistic theory, or from the fact that "progressive specialisation of structure" produces suitability of shape, which by study can be classed under various heads dealing with those characteristics common to occupations, surroundings, and temperaments.

In the accompanying Defence of Cheiromancy I have endeavoured to collect the many facts, both medical and scientific, which can be brought forward to demonstrate that, as the hands are the servants of the system, so all that affects the system affects them. In following out the ideas of many famous men on the subject of the nerve-connection between the brain and the hand, I have in every case given my authority for whatever statement I have adopted. I trust that in this way even the greatest sceptic in such matters will be led to see that the study of the hand has not been confined alone to the attention of those he has so often been pleased to call "weak-minded," but, on the contrary, that men of learning, both among the philosophers of Greece and the scientists of the present, have considered the subject worthy of their time and attention.

When the mysterious action of the brain and its influence over the entire body are considered, it is not surprising to find that those scientists who first proved that there are more nerves between the brain and the hand than in any other portion of the system now go so far with their investigations as even to decide that the brain cannot think without the hand feeling the influence of the thought. It will thus be seen that, viewing palmistry from this standpoint alone, it becomes a study not contrary to the dictates of reason, but in accordance with those natural laws that we observe in the shaping of even inanimate objects, which, by demonstrating the effect of a heretofore cause, are in themselves the cause of a hereafter effect.

In presenting with this work the hands of famous people, I have done so with the object of enabling the student to study the hands of those with whose lives and characteristics he is probably acquainted, and also to show the reader at a glance the difference that exists between the hands of people of different temperaments. It would not be in keeping with the purpose of this book if I were to give a delineation of such hands. In the first place, their owners were too well known to make the readings of value as a test; and in the second, the student will derive greater benefit by tracing out for himself the lines and formations that exhibit each well-known characteristic.

In the following chapters I have endeavoured to place clearly and candidly before the intelligence of the reader the rules and theories that I have proved to be true, and those from whose foundation I have built up whatever success I may have achieved. I have done so for two reasons: the first —and most important—being, that I *believe* in cheiromancy and wish to see it acknowledged as it deserves to be; the second is, that the time is not far distant when, from considerations of health and demands from other fields of labour, I must perforce retire from the scene and leave others—I trust more competent—to take my place.

Nothing has been more removed from my thoughts than the intention of giving offence to any section of the community by any expression, religious or otherwise, contained in these pages. I have, however, used my right of independence of thought and freedom of speech. If, therefore, my remarks should give offence to any sect, community, or people, I am willing to take the responsibility for such statements; but I ask of my accusers that if, in the court of their conscience, my expressions should be condemned, it be on my head alone they hurl their condemnation, and not on the much-maligned study which it has ever been my effort to raise—not to disgrace.

CHEIRO.

NOTE TO THE TWENTY-SEVENTH EDITION

THE twenty-seventh edition of this famous work has been entirely revised and recast to conform to present-day taste and preference. During the course of the work of revision it became apparent that a number of the "hands" of prominent people illustrating the book, and which had served a useful purpose in earlier editions, had now largely lost their significance. It was therefore decided to include none but the quite outstanding from the wide choice of specimens available. One further requirement was added: that the choice be deliberately restricted to the hands of people now dead. This last provision was thought desirable as it would then be possible to view the life of each subject as a completed picture, thus enabling the reader to study the signs, portents and tendencies revealed in the hands and to decide for himself to what extent they were borne out by actual events. To assist the student toward this end, the author has drawn attention in each case to the characteristic points to look for. His comments, however, though excellent as guidance, do nothing to detract from the value of the hands as exercises from the point of view of the reader intent on making his own analyses.

CONTENTS

PART II.—CHEIROMANCY

PART III.—ILLUSTRATIVE TYPES

PART IV

PART V

ILLUSTRATIONS IN LINE

CHEIRO

Count Louis Hamon, 1866-1936, better known to millions as "Cheiro," stood foremost among the world's "seers" for nearly thirty years. Although most famous for his amazing knowledge of palmistry, i.e., "Cheirognomy" and "Cheiromancy," he did not confine himself to any one branch of occult study: numerology and astrology were equally taken into account in his remarkable predictions, and he was a master of all matters relating to the occult.

The world's famous were among his numerous clients. Statesmen, actors, authors, royalty—all beat a path to his door, anxious to have the great Cheiro tell their character, fortune, and future. He traveled all over the world, and wherever he went people eagerly sought his advice. Cheiro also made several extended trips to the United States where many famous personages consulted him, including Mark Twain and Dame Nellie Melba, the great prima donna. He always kept a visitor's book wherein his clients could write their observations about their visit. Nellie Melba, for instance, wrote in his book: "Cheiro you are wonderful—what more can I say?" Mark Twain, who did not "believe" in palmistry, was so impressed by Cheiro's accuracy and insight, that he made use of the science of palmistry in "Pudd'n Head Wilson," a story that enjoyed great success. He wrote in Cheiro's visitor's book: "Cheiro has exposed my character to me with humiliating accuracy. I ought not to confess this accuracy, still I am moved to do so.—Mark Twain."

The Infanta Eulalia of Spain, Sir Arthur Sullivan, the great actress Sarah Bernhardt, Sir Austen Chamberlain—these were just a few of the famous personages who consulted Cheiro. To attest to the importance he attached to Cheiro's predictions, Chamberlain had his hands read in a private room in the House of Commons.

Cheiro's amazing career included many professions. He was also a lecturer and public speaker, war correspondent, editor of newspapers in London and Paris, and successful author of a dozen books on palmistry, numerology, and astrology.

A DEFENCE

The greatest truth may lie in smallest things,
The greatest good in what we most despise,
The greatest light may break from darkest skies,
The greatest chord from e'en the weakest strings.
                                        CHEIRO.

IF any science, art, or work has for its beginning, its object,
and its end the improvement of humanity and the advancement
of the race, then that work, art, or science deserves the encouragement and recognition that is its due.

Of all branches of the study of human nature, that of the
hand has the most powerful claim. By it one can detect, not
only the faults in mankind, but the way in which those faults
may be redeemed. It is the key to that cabinet of character
in which nature conceals not only the motive power necessary
for everyday life, but those latent talents and energies that by
the knowledge of self we can bring to bear upon our lives.

There are few—if any—of us who, looking back upon the
past, will not at some time confess to months, years, and often
the greater part of life's span, that have been lost, through the
fault of parents and our own ignorance combined.

"Know thyself," the motto of the ancients, is the simplest
but the grandest sermon that can ring within our ears. By the
knowledge of nature do we honour nature; let us then consider
the study that can give such knowledge; for by the knowledge
of self may we master self, and by the improvement of self may
we also improve mankind—to the advancement of the race,
to the honour of the world, and to the glory of those who, in
the march of time, will fill life's broken ranks, and some day
take our place.

To endeavour to show the solid and sufficient foundation
that this study rests upon, I will merely ask my readers to follow
the pages of this defence, with curiosity if they wish, but, I
hope, with curiosity tempered by common sense and patience.

It shall therefore be my province to assume the position of the student, and not that of the partisan. Thus, discarding the argumentative standpoint, do I present the history of the study, and the facts upon which it rests, feeling assured that the result will be satisfactory to the reason, the logic, and the common sense of those who, from it matters not what motive, may examine this study for themselves.

To consider the origin of this science, we must take our thoughts back to the earliest days of the world's history, and furthermore to the consideration of a people the oldest of all, yet one that has survived the fall of empires, nations, and dynasties, and who are to-day as characteristic and as full of individuality as they were when thousands of years ago the first records of history were written. I allude to those children of the East, the Hindus, a people whose philosophy and wisdom are every day being more and more revived. Looking back to the earliest days of the history of the known world, we find that the first linguistic records belong to the people under consideration, and date back to that far-distant cycle of time known as the Aryan civilization. Beyond history we cannot go; but the monuments and cave temples of India, according to the testimony of archæologists, all point to a time so far beyond the scant history at our disposal, that in the examination of such matters our greatest knowledge is dwarfed into infantile nothingness—our age and era are but the swaddling-clothes of the child; our manhood that of the infant in the arms of the eternity of time.

In endeavouring to trace the origin of palmistry, we are carried back to the confines of a prehistoric age. History tells us that in the remotest period of the Aryan civilization it had even a literature of its own. Beyond this we cannot go; but as fragments of this literature are even now extant, we must therefore conclude that it had a still more remote infancy; but into that night of antiquity we dare not venture. There are no stars to guide, no faded moons to show us light; and so, standing on the borders of the known, we gaze into the darkness of the unknown, from the vastness of which we occasionally draw the bones of a mammoth or the fragments of a shrine; they are helps to knowledge; they are weeds upon the sands of time; they tell us of days before our days, of races before our race, of verdant islands, of civilization sunk for ever in the ocean of antiquity.

As regards the people who first understood and practised this study of the hand, we find undisputed proofs of their learning and knowledge. Long before Rome or Greece or Israel was even heard of, the monuments of India point back to an age of learning beyond, and still beyond. From the astronomical calculations that the figures in their temples represent, it has been estimated that the Hindus understood the precession of the equinoxes centuries before the Christian era. In some of the ancient cave temples, the mystic figures of the Sphinx silently tell that such knowledge had been possessed and used in advance of all those nations afterward so celebrated for their learning. It has been demonstrated that to make a change from one sign to another in the zodiacal course of the sun must have occupied at the least 2,140 years, and how many centuries elapsed before such changes came to be observed and noticed it is impossible even to estimate.

The intellectual power which was necessary to make such observations speaks for itself; and yet it is to such a people that we trace the origin of the study under consideration. With the spread of the Hindu teachings into other lands do we trace the spread of the knowledge of palmistry. The Hindu Vedas are the oldest scriptures that have been found, and according to some authorities they have been the foundation of even the Greek schools of learning.

When we consider that palmistry is the offspring of such a race, we should for such a reason alone at least treat it with respect, and be more inclined to examine its claims for justice than we are at present. In the examination of these points we therefore find that this study of the hand is one of the most ancient in the world. History again comes to our assistance, and tells that in the north-west province of India, palmistry was practised and followed by the Joshi caste from time immemorial to the present day.

It may be interesting to describe here, in as few words as possible, an extremely ancient and curious book on the markings of hands, which I was allowed to use and examine during my sojourn in India. This book was one of the greatest treasures of the few Brahmans who possessed and understood it, and was jealously guarded in one of those old cave temples that belong to the ruins of ancient Hindustan.

This strange book was made of human skin, pieced and put together in the most ingenious manner. It was of enormous size, and contained hundreds of well-drawn illustrations, with records of how, when, and where this or that mark was proved correct.

One of the strangest features in connection with it was that it was written in some red liquid which age had failed to spoil or fade. The effect of those vivid red letters on the pages of dull yellow skin was most remarkable. By some compound, probably made of herbs, each page was glazed, as it were, by varnish; but whatever this compound may have been, it seemed to defy time, as the outer covers alone showed the signs of wear and decay. As regards the antiquity of this book there could be no question. It was apparently written in three sections or divisions: the first part belonged to the earliest language of the country, and dated so far back that very few of the Brahmans even could read or decipher it. There are many such treasures in Hindustan; but all are so jealously guarded by the Brahmans that neither money, art, nor power will ever release such pledges of the past.

As the wisdom of this strange race spread far and wide across the earth, so the doctrines and ideas of palmistry spread and were practised in other countries. Just as religion suits itself to the conditions of the race in which it is propagated, so has palmistry been divided into systems. The most ancient records, however, are those found among the Hindus. It is difficult to trace its path from country to country. In far-distant ages it has been practised in China, Tibet, Persia, and Egypt; but it is to the days of the Grecian civilization that we owe the present clear and lucid form of the study. The Greek civilization has in many ways been considered the highest and most intellectual in the world, and here it was that palmistry, or cheiromancy—from the Greek *cheir*, the hand—grew, flourished, and found favour in the sight of those whose names are as stars of honour in the firmament of knowledge. We find that Anaxagoras taught and practised it in 423 B.C. We find that Hispanus discovered, on an altar dedicated to Hermes, a book on cheiromancy written in gold letters, which he sent as a present to Alexander the Great, as "a study worthy the attention of an elevated and inquiring mind." We find it also sanctioned by such men of learning as Aristotle, Pliny, Paracelsus, Cardamis, Albertus Magnus, the Emperor Augustus, and many others of note.

Now whether these ancient people were more enlightened than we are, has long been a question of dispute. The point, however, which has been admitted, and the one which concerns this study most, is, that as in those days the greatest study of mankind was man, it therefore follows that in a study like this their conclusions are far more likely to be right than are those of an age famous for its implements of destruction, its steam-engines, and its commerce. Again, if an age like the present will admit, and has admitted, that those Greek philosophers were men of extraordinary depth of thought and learning, and that their works, thoughts, and ideas are worthy of the deepest respect, why should we then lightly consider their authority on this subject, and throw aside a study that so deeply occupied their attention? And again, if we go back, as we do, to these men for their learning in other matters, why, in the name of all that is reasonable, should we reject their knowledge in this?

Now, as in the study of mankind there came to be recognized a natural position on the face for the nose, eyes, ears, etc., so also on the hand there came to be recognized a natural position for the line of head, the line of life, and so on. The time and study devoted to the subject enabled these students to give names to these marks; as the line of head, meaning mentality; the line of heart, affection; the line of life, longevity; and so on, with every mark or mount that the hand possesses. This brings us down to the period when the power of the church was beginning to be felt outside the domain and jurisdiction of religion. It is said that the early Fathers were jealous of the power of this old-world science. Such may or may not have been the case; but even in the present day we find that the church constitutes itself in all matters, both spiritual and temporal, the chosen oracle of God. Without wishing to seem intolerant, one cannot help but remark that the history of any dominant religion is the history of the opposition to knowledge, unless that knowledge proceed from its teachings.

Palmistry, therefore, the child of pagans and heathens, was not even given a trial. It was denounced as rank sorcery and witchcraft. The devil was conjured up as the father of all palmists, and the result was that men and women, terrified to acknowledge such a parentage, allowed palmistry to become outlawed and fall into the hands of vagrants, tramps, and gipsies.

During the Middle Ages several attempts were made to revive this ancient study; as, for instance, *Die Kunst Ciromanta*, published in 1475, and *The Cyromantia Aristotelis cum Figuris*, published 1490, which is at present in the British Museum. These attempts were useful in keeping the ashes of the study from dying out; but it is in the nineteenth century that once more it rises, a Phœnix from the fire of persecution which has tried in vain to destroy it. The science of the present has come to the rescue of the so-called superstition of the past. On almost every side proof is being added to prove that this ancient study is not a delusion, but a real thing—a jewel, as it were, dimmed and covered by the accumulations of bigotry and superstition, yet one which contains within its depths that light of truth which nature's followers delight to know and worship.

It may be well here to defend palmistry from the attacks of the Church. Let us examine for a moment the right of the Church to attack it. Alas! his majesty Satan has still the reputation of being behind every person who dares to advance any science or thought that may not be in accordance with the interpretation of the Church's idea of right and wrong. I had not been in London one month before a Catholic priest refused to give absolution to an entire family because they had consulted me against his orders. In America, during my first year, I was visited by two clergymen, with the object of persuading me that my success was due alone to the agency of the devil. One went so far as to tell me that God had sent him to offer me a clerkship—at a small salary, of course—if I would only give up my relations with the Evil One. But all this is not to be wondered at when one remembers that in one of the most prominent churches in America, a very noted clergyman used these words:

"Let me tell you what I saw a few years ago with my own

eyes." Then followed a long description of "a fiery animal shaped like a horse, that glowed like a burning coal, which had a man mounted upon it without arms. It rolled from one end of the island to the other, and from side to side with immense speed. The people were terrified; they thought it was the devil, and they implored me to intercede for them, but I refused. . . . I have travelled all over the world and seen the greatest sights and wonders of the earth; but I never saw anything like that before. It was a warning to all who saw it, and represented Satan and his army, who are to visit with awful results the sinners of the earth."

I make no comment. I quote the above words verbatim from a leading New York paper, which reported the entire sermon.

The Church is not consistent; its foundation is the Bible, and from the first of Genesis to the end of Revelation the Bible is a book of fate. In the opening chapters we find that God ordained a certain time when a virgin would conceive, and a little later when a Judas would betray. Poor Judas thus becomes a selected victim, a child of fate, from whom opportunities would arise to alter the destiny of nations. It is useless to say that Judas was a free agent; if he had shirked his fate would not some other man have had to take his place "that the Scriptures might be fulfilled"? Over fourteen times in the Gospels do we find these mysterious words. In almost every portion of the Bible we find the spirit of prophecy encouraged. We find "Schools of the Prophets" established for such a purpose, and indications that divinations were held in high repute by God's chosen people. Among the Hebrews, as among the Hindus, Egyptians, Chaldeans, and all nations who encouraged the spirit of prophecy, the prophets were a separate and distinct class from the priesthood. Among the Jews the prophets often acted in direct opposition to the priesthood, denouncing in the strongest language the abominations and corruptions that they practised. Again, what can be more mystical, or more allied to magic, than the ancient cabbala of the Jews? According to tradition it was communicated by God to Adam, by Adam given to Seth, and lost by the latter in some mysterious way. It was renewed again by God to Moses on Mount Sinai, from Moses to Joshua, from Joshua to the

Seventy Elders, and was sometimes utilised by learned Jews instead of the counsels of the Talmud. Examining the Biblical statement that the Jews were in bondage to Egypt at a time when the Egyptians were famous for their magic, it cannot be wondered at that after leaving that land of mystery they would still cling to the teachings imbibed while there. According to many authorities, the description of the Hebrews despoiling the Egyptians on the eve of their departure, and robbing them of their ornaments, signifies in cabbalistic language "the taking from them the external rites and ceremonials of their magical worship." We therefore find that the Bible, upon which the creeds of the modern Church are founded, is tinged with the mysticism common to its time; that it encourages prophecy, and that it teaches fate: which three things in the study of palmistry arouse the wrath of the Church, and are denounced as sorcery, witchcraft, and everything else contrary to the teaching of God.

In view of the opposition of the Church, it is interesting to notice the many important phrases in the Bible in which hands are mentioned. There are many authorities who affirm that among the arts learned by the Jews while in Egypt was this study of the hand; but the most important verse that is used in support of this is the seventh of the thirty-seventh chapter of Job. In the original Hebrew it appears to have a very different meaning from that given to it by the English version. One translation of it runs, "God placed signs or seals in the hands of men, that all men might know their works." This verse, about the middle of the sixteenth century, caused some very great discussions among theologians and commentators. Among them we find that many advocated the cheiromantic aspect that the lines of the hand are "the markings of God, that all men might know their works." Among those in support of this view were Franciscus Valesius, Schultens, Lyrannus, Thomassin, and Debrio, and this is all the more remarkable when one remembers that these men could not have lived in a more antagonistic age in which to propagate their views. The translation of the Bible into English at a time when the opposition to palmistry, sorcery, and witchcraft was at its height, is very probably the cause of the wording of this verse as it now stands.

Among other verses that seem to bear a relation to this point might be mentioned:

"Length of days is in her right hand, riches and honour are in her left" (Prov. iii. 16).

"What evil is in mine hand?" (1 Sam. xxvi. 18).

"And receive his mark in his forehead, or in his hand" (Rev. xiv. 9).

But of all the many allusions to the subject, the verse in Job is certainly the most important and one which, as I have shown, has called forth the support of even theologians.

In connection with the opposition of the Church, the most absurd point, to my mind, is that this very Church does not hesitate to preach fate for another world while determinedly tabooing such a doctrine as regards this. There are a great many sects who openly advocate the doctrine of predestination as far as religious matters are concerned. What is known as the English Church goes so far as to make it one of her articles of faith, as in the seventeenth Article of Religion, where it is stated that "predestination to life is the everlasting purpose of God, whereby, before the foundations of the world were laid, He hath decreed by His counsel secret to us," to do this, that, or the other, according to the ideas of the learned gentlemen who framed the article.

To deal thus with an eternity of life, thus to plan out the political economy of that which is unknown, is a thousand times more unreasonable than to ask people to believe that *as the hands are the servants of the system, so all things which affect the system affect them.* It is strange, but it is a fact that the people who believe the most extraordinary theories as regards religion are the very people who cry out that it is absurd to believe in any study like this of palmistry. Surely this is not consistent.

We will now see what science has done for palmistry, and whether or not it has any foundation beyond that of mere speculation and hypothesis. In this age of specialism which is so characteristic of the present century, we find in almost all departments of life men devoting their time to some one particular branch of study. In past ages it was common for a man to be a physician, a chemist, and a surgeon combined. There was, in fact, no limit to the things to which he might turn his attention. In the nineteenth century, however, and particularly towards its close, we found specialists arising in all directions. A surgeon need not practise as a physician, nor a physician as a surgeon; a dentist need not be a doctor, and a chemist need not be a bone-setter. Particularly in science is this change seen, and with very astonishing results in the independent discoveries and improvements that have been made.

This specialisation has, however, one very great evil. It may give greater knowledge on particular things, but it confines men to a narrower line of thought. It therefore happens that the physician may know little about anatomy, whereas the surgeon may know next to nothing of medicine; the nerve specialist won't treat the common ailments of life, and the doctor will not infringe upon the latter; the physician who devotes his talents to consumption cures won't treat fever patients; and so on. Now all this leads up to a very grave point, namely, the unreasonable way in which the ordinary populace treat the ordinary medical man. A man sees, perhaps, a strange experiment in hypnotism; he goes to his physician, and because that physician, who probably has never devoted five minutes' study to such a subject, pronounces such a thing impossible, the patient goes away and tells his acquaintances to pooh-pooh the idea, because Dr. So-and-so does not believe in it. Now, when one considers that even in medicine there are hundreds of mysteries perfectly unknown to the ordinary medical man, how much more so may it not be in regard to the mysteries of life and nature, which are subject to invisible laws beyond the power of man to analyse?

I respect doctors as a body of educated men; but I do not respect the idea that they should be the appointed judges of such matters as telepathy, mesmerism, clairvoyance, and so on, without any other qualification but that of having M.D. to their name. It was Voltaire who said that "Newton, with all his science, did not know how his hand moved." Almost every day in my work, the following conversation occurs:

"Well, sir, you have told me the events of my past life so accurately from these lines that I am half-inclined to believe you *can* tell the future; but I have asked Dr. So-and-so; he says it must be all humbug, so I really do not know what to think." Alas! Dr. So-and-so too often turns out to be a man who has never had the time, the opportunity, or even the inclination to study the connection between the brain and the hand. He has not even read the works of medical specialists on the subject. He has confined himself to the treatment of fever, pneumonia, the illnesses of children, or the hypochondriacal fads and fancies of age. He knows that there are such things as hands, that they are dry and hot during fever, and that is about all.

In reference to this I quote a few remarks from the address of the president of the New Jersey State Medical Society, in which he said:

"How many physicians know *anything* of the natural cause of most diseases except by hearsay? How many have had the courage to observe for themselves while sternly combating the seductive opportunity of prescribing a variety of unnecessary medicines?"

Not more than twenty years ago almost every physician of note cried out that hypnotism was impossible. To-day the same profession embraces it, and studies the very laws whose existence it once denied. It is the same with cheiromancy: for years they have pooh-poohed the idea; to-day they admit that diseases are indicated in a marvellous manner by the hand, and at present the study of the shape of the nails is a branch calling forth the greatest attention from medical men in both London and Paris.

If the medical profession could only forget their old-time prejudices; if they could only be persuaded to take some reliable work on palmistry and study it for themselves—they would without doubt come to the conclusion that, in the words of Hispanus, it was indeed "a study worthy the attention of an elevated and inquiring mind."

In relation to this I publish the following letter which appeared in the *Student*, a paper belonging to the University of Edinburgh, Scotland.

CHEIROMANCY

SIR: Some years ago I was walking through one of the wards in the Royal Infirmary when suddenly the idea occurred to me that I would examine the lines on a patient's hand.

I went to the nearest bed, and without pausing to look at the patient, I examined his hand. I knew little of palmistry, and believed still less; in fact, I hardly knew more than the names of the five principal lines, and that breaks in those lines meant misfortune. I examined the hands, and saw the life-line broken in both hands, and the fate-line, before it had reached a quarter of its natural length, stopped and replaced by a large cross. I questioned the patient, and found that he was twenty-three years old, and far gone in phthisis. He died in a few days. I could multiply instances, but space forbids. Would you then allow me to offer a few suggestions as to the possible relation of these lines to processes carried on in the cells of the grey matter? I am well aware that palmistry is considered quackery and humbug; but, after all, facts are stubborn things, even if they do not rest on any *known* scientific basis.

[A few suggestions on the possible relation of linear markings on the palm of the hand to certain physiological and psychical processes in the brain.]

1.   The hand is a high stage of development peculiar to man as a reasonable being.

2.   Tendencies, such as eloquence, anger, and affection, are shown by movements.

3.   These movements are coarse and fine, and so produce large and small creases or lines.

4.   Creases and lines, therefore, bear a definite relation to movements, and so to tendencies.

5.   There are four well-marked creases or lines on every hand, found by experience to bear a definite relation to the tendencies of affection, mental capacity, longevity, and mental bent, or what cheiromants call "fate."

6.   A line crossing the longevity line. a branch or break in it, interferes with its uniformity, and therefore interferes with the uniformity of the tendency to live.

7.   Nerves regulating coarser and finer motions, and so creases or lines, contain chiefly motor fibres; but probably also other filaments transmitting in vibrations the resultant or combined effect of acquired and constitutional tendencies, and determining it to that part of the longevity line that will be affected, and there causing a crease resembling a cross by its junction with the main line or a branch, as the case may be.

8.   The same train of reasoning obviously applies to *avoidable accidents*—that is, accidents caused by carelessness.

9.   *Unavoidable accidents.* Certain tracts of cells in the conical grey matter are, incredible as it may seem, probably affected by coming events, and made to vibrate; hence, vague fears, intuitive perception, but no actual train of reasoning. The vibrations excited in these cells cannot awaken the activity of the cells engaged in

reasoning processes that adjoins them, but merely cause protoplasmic vibrations in them, these vibrations being transmitted and marked on the hand by creases of different shapes. According to cheiromants, the left hand is what you are, constitutionally; the right hand, what you make yourself or acquire. We may, therefore, reasonably expect to see in the right hand the resultant of acquired and constitutional tendencies.

As regards futurity, I think it not impossible that Professor Charcot's researches on the higher functions of the nervous system will demonstrate that tracts of cells, or a pathological condition of these cells, enables a perception of futurity, but no memory of it.

(Signed) SPERANUS.

It will thus be seen that it requires but a little study of the subject to convince even the most sceptical that "there is something in the lines"; and if a little, why not a great deal, if a sufficient amount of study be devoted to it?

In medical work, hœmatoma of the ear has been for a long time recognized. This consists in the upper portion of the ear assuming a peculiar shape, either by the formation of a blood tumour, or by the thickening of the upper portion, which is found in the ears of lunatics, generally those who inherit madness; but in Paris it was much more closely studied, with the result that tests were given before the Académie des Sciences, proving that madness could be predicted years in advance by a proper study of the ear alone. Now my argument is, that if, as has been proved, accurate prediction can be made by a study of the ear, is there then anything impossible in prediction being far more accurately made by a study of the hand, which has been pronounced to be, both in nerves and mechanism, the most wonderful organ in the entire system, and to have the most intimate connection with the brain?

Almost all medical men admit now that the different formations of nails indicate different diseases, and that it is possible from the nails alone to predict that the subject will suffer from paralysis, consumption, heart disease, and so on. Many a well-known doctor has told me that he has read more from the hand than he dared acknowledge, and that it was but the old-time prejudices which kept many a man from admitting the same thing.

At this point let me also draw a comparison between the

way a doctor treats his patient and the way a palmist
treats his client. I draw this comparison on account of
the unfair manner in which medical men as a rule treat the
palmist.

In the first place, the doctor has a recognized science to
go by; he has scientific instruments with the most modern
improvements to assist his researches; but how many can tell
the patient what he is suffering from, unless the patient first
tells the doctor all about himself and his symptoms; and even
then, how often can the doctor arrive at a correct diagnosis?
Some readers may have heard that during the great epidemic
of *La Grippe* in London, many years ago, letters appeared in
the leading papers relating to the experiences of a man who
visited seven of the most noted physicians of the day; that these
seven, after thoroughly examining him, each said he was
suffering from a different disease, and all prescribed entirely
different drugs for him to take.

Now, in the case of a palmist, the client, without giving his
or her name, without telling his occupation, or whether married
or single, simply holds out his hands, and the palmist has to
tell him past events in his life, present surroundings, health
past and present; and having, by accuracy only, gained his con-
fidence, he proceeds to read the future from the same materials
that he has told the past. Now, if the palmist, without
one particle of the help that the doctor gets, should make one
mistake, the client immediately considers that he is a charlatan,
and palmistry a delusion and a snare. If, however, the doctor
makes a blunder, it is never known, but the result is that the
patient has been "called away by Providence to another
sphere."

I leave my readers to draw their own conclusions.

Among the testimony and ideas given by scientific men we
find the greatest possible arguments in favour of the cheiromantic use of the lines, formations, mounts, and so forth. In
the first place, the markings of no two hands have ever been
found alike. This is particularly noticeable in the case of
twins; the lines will be widely different if the natures are different in their individuality, but at least some important difference
will be shewn, in accordance with the different temperaments.
It has also been noted that even with the lines of the hand a

certain peculiarity will run in families for generations, and that each succeeding race will also show in temperament whatever that peculiar characteristic is. But again, it will be found that in the markings of the hand some children bear very little resemblance, in the position of the lines, to those of the parents, and that, if one watches their lives, they will, in accordance with this theory, be found very different from those who gave them birth. Again, one child may resemble the father, another the mother, and the markings of the hand will also be found to correspond with the markings on the hand of the particular parent that the child resembles.

It is a very popular fallacy that the lines are made by work. The direct opposite, however, is the case. At the birth of the infant the lines are deeply marked (Plate IX). Work, on the contrary, covers the hand with a coarse layer of skin, and so hides instead of exposes them; but if the hand is softened, by poulticing or other means, the entire multitude of marks will be shown at any time from the cradle to the grave.

The superiority of the hand is well worth our attention. Scientists and men of learning in all ages have agreed that it plays one of the most important parts of all the members of the body. Anaxagoras has said: "The superiority of man is owing to his hands." In Aristotle's writings we find: "The hand is the organ of organs, the active agent of the passive powers of the entire system." More recently, such men as Sir Richard Owen, Humphrey, and Sir Charles Bell all call attention to the importance of the hand. Sir Charles Bell wrote: "We ought to define the hand as belonging exclusively to man, *corresponding, in its sensibility and motion, to the endowment of his mind.*"

Sir Richard Owen, in his work on *The Nature of Limbs*, said: "In the hand every single bone is distinguishable from one another; each digit has its own peculiar character."

It has long been known and recognised that the hand can express almost as much by its gestures and positions as the lips can by speech. Quintilian, speaking of the language of hands, says: "For the other parts of the body assist the speaker, but these, I may say, speak for themselves; they ask, they promise, they invoke, they dismiss, they threaten, they entreat, they deprecate, they express fear, joy, grief, our doubts, our assents, our penitence, they show moderation, profusion, they mark number and time."

We will now give our attention to the skin, the nerves, and the sense of touch. Speaking of the skin, Sir Charles Bell once said: "The cuticle is so far a part of the organ of touch that it is the medium through which the external impression is conveyed to the nerve. The extremities of the fingers best exhibit the provisions for the exercise of this sense. The nails give support to the tips of the fingers, and in order to sustain the elastic cushion that forms their extremities they are made broad and shield-like. This cushion is an important part of the exterior apparatus. Its fullness and elasticity adapt it admirably for touch. It is a remarkable fact that we cannot feel the pulse with the tongue, *but that we can with the fingers.* On a nearer inspection we discover in the points of the fingers a more particular provision for adapting them to touch. Wherever the sense of feeling is most exquisite, there we see minute spiral ridges of the cuticle. These ridges have corresponding depressions on the inner surface, and they again give lodgement to soft, pulpy processes of the skin called papillæ, in which lie the extremities of the sentient nerves. Thus the nerves are adequately protected, while they are at the same time sufficiently exposed to have impressions communicated to them through the elastic cuticle and thus give rise to the sense of touch."

As regards the nerves, medical science has demonstrated that the hand contains more nerves than any other portion of the system, and the palm contains more than any other portion of the hand. It has also been shown that the nerves from the brain to the hand are so highly developed by generations of use, that the hand, whether passive or active, is in every sense the immediate servant of the brain. A very interesting medical work states "that every apparent single nerve is in reality two nerve cords in one sheath; the one conveys the action of the brain to the part, and the other conveys the action of the part to the brain."

In connection with this, it is important to consider the corpuscles that are found in the hand. Meissner, in his *Anatomy and Physiology of the Hand,* showed that these corpuscles in the hand have a very important meaning. He demonstrated that these "unyielding molecular substances" were found in the tips of the fingers, the lines of the hand, and disappeared completely at the wrist; that these corpuscles contained the end of the important nerve fibre, and during the life of the body gave forth certain crepitations or vibrations, which ceased the moment life became extinct. "I have counted," says he, "in the first phalange of the volar surface of the forefinger of a full-grown man, one hundred and eight corpuscles, and about four hundred papillæ in a square line."

These investigations were afterwards followed up by experiments as to the noises or crepitations that they gave forth during life. It was demonstrated that people with acute hearing could detect these vibrations distinct and different in every human being. And in the case of a man experimented on in Paris, who was born blind, but whom nature had compensated by giving him a greater sense of hearing, it was found that by listening to the vibrations of these corpuscles "he could determine the sex, age, and temperament, the state of health, and even their nearness to illness and death."

We will now turn our attention to what, perhaps, as far as palmistry is concerned, may be the most important point of all, namely, as to the ideas of men of learning as regards a fluid or essence in connection with the nerves and the brain.

On this point Abercrombie stated: "The communication of perceptions from the senses to the mind has been accounted for by motions of the nervous fluid, by vibrations of the nerves, or by a subtle essence resembling electricity or galvanism." We find that this theory has been very freely circulated by those who have devoted serious thought to the subject. Müller also said: "Perhaps there exists between the phenomena of the nervous system and of electricity a sympathy or connection at present unknown, analogous to that which has been found to exist between electricity and magnetism." And again he said: "We know not *as yet* whether or no, when the nerves convey an impression, an imponderable fluid flies along them with inconceivable rapidity, or whether the action of the nervous system consists of an imponderable principle already existent in the nerves, and placed in vibration by the brain."

I had the honour of knowing personally Professor Savary d'Odiardi, a well-known French savant who devoted the greater part of his life to investigating the curative effect of electricity in disease. The astounding cures made by this man, through his knowledge of the part that electricity plays in daily life, made him one of the greatest living authorities on the subject of his time.

During a conversation I had with him he also stated that he considered the nerves a kind of telegraph system in conveying the current of thought from the brain to the body, but more especially in their connection and relation to the hand.

Herder, in his *Idées sur la Philosophie de l'Histoire de l'Humanité*, published Paris, 1827, wrote also in favour of this theory. He spoke of the action of the nervous fluid, which he taught is an essence far more subtle than that of electricity, and used to convey the impressions of the brain to the nerves. All such opinions from well-known men who devoted time and thought to the subject go far to show that the influence of the mind in this or that direction must affect the lines, the nails, and in fact every portion of the hand. There is nothing superstitious in such a theory; it is based upon the findings of science, and has been supported by facts that are undisputed. After all, why should it be otherwise? According to eminent authorities we find that "in the examination of a skeleton, a zoologist recognizes that the irregularities and ridges found upon the surface of the bones are the result of the action and pressure of muscles and nerves"; that from the broken fragment of a bone the scientist can build up the entire structure and proportions of the dead animal, his race, habits, and even the diseases he would be liable to. If such can be done from the fragment of a bone, looking at the subject from this standpoint alone, how much, I ask, may we not do by a careful study of the most important member of the body—the hand? Is there anything absurd or ridiculous in the idea that the hand specialist (as the true palmist is) should attempt and be able to read the health, the surroundings of the past and present, and even the future, from an examination of the hand, independent of any palmistic theory of lines to go by?

That the lines are not produced by work we have noted earlier. If, therefore, as has been demonstrated, they are not produced by work, they likewise are not produced by constant folding. It is true that the hands fold on the lines, but it is also true that lines and marks are found where no folding can possibly take place, and if so in one case, why not in all? Again, there are many diseases (as, for example, paralysis) in which the lines completely disappear, although the hands continue to fold as before. The folding argument, it will therefore be observed, does not hold ground.

As regards the question: Is the study of phrenology and physiognomy to be considered as an aid in a cheiromantic examination?—a little thought will convince the inquirer that such is not by any means necessary. A thorough study of the hand will combine both. The hand, by its direct communication with every portion of the brain, tells not only the qualities active, but those dormant, and those which will be developed. As regards physiognomy, the face allows itself to be too easily controlled to be accurate in its findings, but the lines cannot be altered to suit the purposes of the moment.

It is Balzac who has said, in his *Comédie Humainé*: "We acquire the faculty of imposing silence upon our lips, upon our eyes, upon our eyebrows, and upon our foreheads; the hand alone does not dissemble—no feature is more expressive than the hand."

We will now turn to the question of the future as revealed by this study, and carefully examine the reasons advanced for such a belief.

In the first place, we must bear in mind that the meaning of the different lines in conjunction with the different types of hands dates back to that period already referred to when this study lay in the hands of men who devoted their lives to its cultivation. Now, as there came to be recognized a natural position for the nose or the lips on the face, so in the study of the hand there came to be recognized a natural position for the line of head or the line of life, as the case might be. How such a thing was originally discovered is not our province to determine, but that the truth of such designations has been proved, and can be proved, will be admitted by any person who will even casually examine hands for himself. Therefore, if proved in one point that certain marks on the line of head mean this or that mental peculiarity, or that certain marks on the line of life have relation to length of life or the reverse, the same course of observation, it is not illogical to assume, can predict illness, health, madness, and death. If persisted in, it may be also accurate in its observation that marriage will occur at this or that point, with this or that result, and also in regard to prosperity or the reverse. It is beyond my power to answer why such a thing should be, but it is surely not beyond my jurisdiction to advance the following theory: That as the hidden laws of nature become more revealed by each century of time, so does man become more cognizant of the fact that things before called mysteries are but produced by the action of certain laws that beforetime he was ignorant of. I also advance the theory that it is not possible for us to lead the isolated lives that at first sight appear probable; that as the laws which affect the entire universe affect us, so do we, as part of a whole, *affect again those laws, and thus one another.* In examining this question we find that the hand preaches, to a certain extent, the doctrine of fate, in its prediction of things years in advance, and in its relation to the effect of circumstances over which we have little or no control. There is here, however, a strange combination, not only interesting but instructive: man appears responsive to the dual laws of destiny and free will. Man has free will, I argue, but with limitations, as there are limitations to all other things in life—to one's strength, to one's height, to one's age, and so forth. Free will is the *oscillation of the cylinder, which very oscillation drives the eternal machinery of evolution.* Looking over the pages of the Bible, we find destiny absolute, the purpose of God appearing in all things. Looking back over the history of the world, the fate of nations stands out in grand relief upon the sombre background of the past. Man becomes the servant of destiny. The rulers of Rome, the Grecians of Athens, the Pharaohs of the Nile, all have served their purpose and are gone. We behold in all the slow but steady stride of evolution bearing us higher, bearing us to perfection. Let us look back—the lessons of the past may be the teachers of the future. We behold an age when freedom of thought lay dying beneath the dogma of a Church; we behold a bondage great as any when a Rama rose in Hindustan, a Moses in Egypt, or a Christ in Jerusalem; a million things lead to the one crisis—again history is repeated, again a man is forced to the front. Was there anything in the appearance of that insignificant monk, Luther, that he should be called upon

to take such a responsibility upon his shoulders? Ah! he was
not called upon by man, destiny was again absolute—nature
was one-sided, the balance had to be restored. God—nature—
fate—we will not quarrel about a name—working through the
medium of hereditary laws, so fashioned a man that, standing
in the niche of necessity, he was the lever upon which the fate
of thousands depended. The same in the case of Napoleon,
the same again in the boy George Washington, and as in the
greater, so in the smaller; from creed to creed, from class to
class, from the President to the preacher, from the banker to
the gamin, all fulfil their purpose, each star within its sphere,
each person, each position, all are chords and discords, notes
and harmonies in the song of life, and as in the ultimate
millenium of perfection will that perfection be eternal, so shall
all share the perfection of that grand harmony of which even
now we form the tones, the semi-tones, and the discords.

Is it hard to believe in some unseen law, some mysterious
cause or power that thus shapes and controls our lives? If at
first sight it seems so, we must consider the hundred and one
things we have believed in with less foundation. To be consistent, we must remember the multitudinous variety of reli-
gions, creeds, and theories that have not only been accepted by
the masses, but have been the solid beliefs of intellectual minds.
If, therefore, people can so easily believe in that which is beyond
this state of life, of which no actual facts exist, is there anything
so very absurd in supporting a doctrine of fate, which it is
logical to suppose exists, if we only take it from the standpoint
of the repetition of events from natural causes? On this
question I would draw attention to the words of Dugald Stewart
in his *Outlines of Moral Philosophy*, in which he says: "All
philosophical inquiry, and all that practical knowledge which
guides our conduct in life presupposes such an established
order in the succession of events as enables us to form conjec-
tures *concerning the future from the observation of the past.*"

Man therefore becomes both the maker and the servant of
destiny, bringing into force, by his existence alone, certain
laws that react upon himself, and, through him, upon others.
The present is therefore the effect of a heretofore cause; and
again, *the present is the cause of a hereafter effect.* The deeds
of the past are the karma of the present, as in "the sins of the

fathers," and in the effect of hereditary laws. As we, therefore, work out our own fate, so do we make fate for those to follow, and so on in every degree from stage to stage in the world's progress.

It will thus be seen that instead of this doctrine becoming a dangerous one, it becomes the reverse. It forces men and women to realize the *responsibility of life*: it teaches them to feel for others, and not to be careful alone for the salvation of self. This creed I hold would suit all classes of the community, would raise men by its unselfishness, would redeem them by its personal claim, would broaden men's views, that where now they see but dogma they would see Truth; would teach that we, the children of humanity, being brothers and sisters, should serve one another, to the ultimate perfection of the race, to the benefit of all life, and to the advancement of those who are yet to come.

This doctrine of fate does not retard men from work, it advances them on the plane of work. It does not hold out a reward for work done, which, after all, is but the wage of the hireling; it gives the higher satisfaction of doing one's best, that others may be better—no more. It teaches patience in trial, resignation in affliction, humbleness in success, and virtue in whatever position in life "it has pleased God (or fate) to call us."

Contrast this doctrine with that of free will as usually preached, and what is the result? We find the greatest man reduced to the smallest atom in the immensity of humanity. We look lower in the scale of life, we see millions of beings crushing one another, living on one another, struggling with all the fierceness of their freedom. There is no contentment in such a scene, no peace, no beauty; not even in their religion do we find the rest which after death should be the reward of the weary.

On the other hand, the true fatalist will not close his hands and wait, he will open them and work, earnestly and patiently and well, remembering that the burden he bears has been made for him to teach him to make lighter the burdens of others. He will feel that he is a link in life's chain, which is eternal; that no matter how small that link may be, it still has its purpose —to be borne with patience, to be served with honour. 'Tis

naught to him the clash of creeds, 'tis naught the success of
the moment, or the failure of the year; he will do wrong in
his life, as well as right—we all do; evil is as necessary as good—
but he will do his best, that is all. And at the end—well,
there is no end, for even if there be no life beyond, he lives
again in the particles of clay from whence he came; but if there
be a spirit, then is his spirit part of the eternal spirit of all
things, and so in the success of all is he successful. This is,
to my mind, the doctrine of fate as preached by this study of
the hand; this is the creed that has been despised by the
church and ranked as "an enemy to the teachings of God."
What that agency or power is which marks the hands may for
ever remain a mystery, but that does not qualify us for obstin-
ately refusing to believe in it—because *we* do not know. A
man might as well say, "I refuse to live, because I do not know
all that constitutes life," or "I refuse to think, because I do not
know the process of thought."   There are hundreds of mysteries, even in the simple things of life, that the finite mind
cannot fathom, but we cannot afford to discard them because
we do not know their cause.   The greatest thinkers, Christian
or anti-Christian, have acknowledged their belief in some power
beyond our control, that "shapes our ends, rough hew them how
we will."   What can be stronger than the words of Professor
Tyndall: "Life and its conditions set forth the operations of
an inscrutable power; we know not its origin, we know not its
end; the presumption, if not the degradation, rests with those
who place upon the throne of the universe a magnified image of
themselves."

Voltaire has said: "There is a power that acts within us
without consulting us."

And lastly, let me draw attention to the words of Emerson:
"A little consideration of what takes place around us every
day must show us that *a higher law than that of our will regulates
events*."

We have now seen how this study has survived from age
to age. We have seen how even hard-headed materialistic
science brings forth facts to support its theories. We have
viewed it from a natural light, and we find it natural; we have
examined it from a religious standpoint, and it is religious; we
find that good can be done through it, not only in its doctrines

of the responsibility of life, but in its warnings, in its cautions, and in the knowledge of self that it gives to all. What, then, is to be done? Discard it, because of opposition? No, we must help it for the sake of the truth that it possesses. We must teach it to others, that its knowledge may be power. We must use it because of its use, we must support it because of its support; and lastly, to the man or woman who, in spite of reason, of proofs, of facts, still doubts—to such a person, using Foster's argument against atheism as a foundation, I would say, that by taking such a position they do not do themselves justice as reasonable or intellectual beings. And why? Because unless they know every law that controls mankind, that law that they do not know may be the one whose existence they deny. Unless they have been in every portion of the universe, that portion they have not seen may contain the secret of the whole; and unless they know every power that constitutes life, that power they do not know may be the very one that marks the hand.

PART I: CHEIROGNOMY

CHAPTER I

OF THE SHAPES OF HANDS AND FINGERS

PALMISTRY should really mean the study of the hand in its entirety. It is, however, divided into two sections: the twin sciences of cheirognomy and cheiromancy. The first deals with the shape of the hand and fingers, and relates to the hereditary influence of character and disposition; and the second to the lines and markings of the palm, to the events of past, present, and future.

It will therefore be readily understood that the second portion of this study cannot be complete without the first; and as in the study, so in the reading of the hand—the student should first observe the shape and formation, skin, nails, etc., before proceeding to judge the lines and markings of the palm. Some people consider this portion of the subject too uninteresting to merit much attention, and books on palmistry frequently ignore its importance, and commence too quickly with the more interesting details of cheiromancy.

A little thought will, however, convince the student that such a plan is a mistake, and can only result in error; that if the subject is worth any study at all, it is certainly worth going into thoroughly; besides, the shape of the hand can be more readily observed than the lines of the palm, and it is therefore all the more interesting, as by this means one can read the character of strangers while sitting in the railway train, the church, the concert, or the salon.

The characteristics of various nations as shown by the shape of the hand is also a fascinating branch of the study, and one very much neglected. Later, I will endeavour to point out the leading characteristics that I myself have observed in relation to this portion of the subject. The varying shape of hands and their suitability to various kinds of occupation is also worthy of note, and although by the exercise of will we can alter and make up, in a certain degree, for almost any constitutional defect, yet it is undoubtedly the case that certain types are more suited for one work than another, which it is the more immediate province of cheirognomy to determine. We will therefore at once proceed to consider the different types of hands with their various modifications, in their relation to temperament and character.

There are seven types of hands, each of which may again be subdivided into seven varieties.

The seven types are:

I.   The elementary, or the lowest type.
II. The square, or the useful hand.
III. The spatulate, or the nervous active type.
IV. The philosophic, or the knotty hand.
V.   The conic, or the artistic type.
VI. The psychic, or the idealistic hand.
VII. The mixed hand.

The seven varieties are formed by the blending of the seven types. Among civilized nations the elementary being rarely found in its purity, we therefore commence with the square, divided into seven heads, as, for example: the square with square fingers, short; the square with square fingers, long; the square with knotty fingers; the square with spatulate fingers; the square with conic fingers; the square with psychic fingers; and the square with mixed fingers.

CHAPTER II

THE ELEMENTARY, OR LOWEST TYPE

THIS hand naturally belongs to the lowest type of mentality. In appearance it is coarse and clumsy, with large, thick, heavy palm, short fingers, and short nails (Fig. 1). It is always important to notice the length of the palm and fingers. Some books on palmistry state that to show intellectuality the fingers should always be longer than the palm; but an examination of this statement will show that it is not correct. It has not been proved that fingers have been found longer than the palm. That they may be nearly as long, or as long, there can be no doubt; but it is a very rare case to find them even of the same length. When, however, in proportion to the size of the palm the fingers are long, it indicates a more intellectual nature than when they are short. In Dr. Cairn's work on the physiognomy of the human body, he states that "the bones of the palm form, among brute animals, almost the whole hand." The deduction, therefore, is that the more the palm dominates the hand, the more does the animal nature rule. This is the important point in the elementary hand: the palm is always thick and coarse, and the fingers short and clumsy. There are also very few lines to be seen on the palm. The people possessing such a type have very little mental capacity, and what they do possess leans more to the order of the brute. They have little or no control over their passions; love of form, colour, and beauty does not appeal to them. The thumb of such hands is short and thick, with the upper part or nail phalange heavy, full, and generally square. Such people are violent in temper, passionate but not courageous. If they commit murder, it is in the fury and in the spirit of destruction. They possess a certain low cunning, but the cunning of instinct, not reason. These are people without aspirations; they but eat, drink, sleep, and die. (See also "The Hands of Nations," Chapter XVI.)

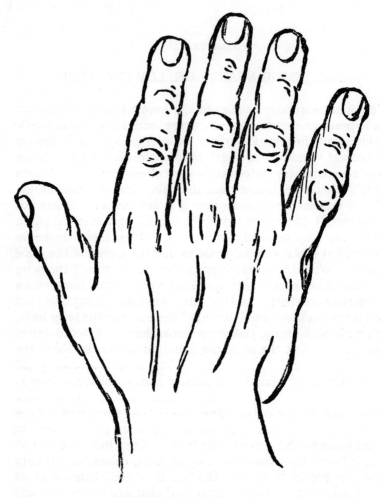

THE ELEMENTARY HAND

Fig. 1

CHAPTER III

THE SQUARE HAND AND ITS SUBDIVISIONS

THE square hand means the palm square at the wrist, square at the base of the fingers, and the fingers themselves square (Fig. 2). Such a type is also called the useful, because it is found in so many walks of life. With this type the nails as well are generally short and square.

People with such a hand are orderly, punctual, and precise in manner, not, however, from any innate grace of nature, but more from conformity with custom and habit. They respect authority, they love discipline, they have a place for everything and everything is kept in its place, not only in their household, but in their brains. They respect law and order, and are slaves to custom; they are not quarrelsome, but are determined in opposition; they prefer reason to instinct, peace to war, and are methodical in work and in habit. They are endowed with great perseverance, but are tenacious, not resigned; they are not enthusiastic over poetry or art; they ask for the material, they win success in practical things. In religion they will not go to extremes; they prefer substance to show, and dogma to ideas. They are not adaptable to people, or versatile; they have little originality or imagination, but in work they have great application, force of character, strength of will, and often outdistance their more brilliant and talented rivals. They naturally love the exact sciences, and all practical study. They encourage agriculture and commerce; they love home and the duties of home, but are not demonstrative in affection. They are sincere and true in promises, staunch in friendship, strong in principle, and honest in business. Their greatest fault is that they are inclined to reason by a twelve-inch rule, and disbelieve all they cannot understand.

THE SQUARE HAND WITH SHORT SQUARE FINGERS

This peculiarity is very often found, and very easily recognized. The subject with such a type is materialistic in every sense of the term. He would be the kind of man who would say: "Except I hear with my ears and see with my eyes, I cannot believe." And even then I very much doubt if such a man would be convinced. It also denotes an obstinate kind of nature, as a rule, narrow-minded. These people make money, but by plodding; they may not be miserly, but they are business-like and practical; they like to accumulate wealth; it is the material they seek.

THE SQUARE HAND WITH LONG SQUARE FINGERS

The next modification is the square hand with very long fingers. This denotes a greater development of mentality than the square hand with short fingers. It denotes logic and method, but in a greater degree than possessed by the purely square type, which, tied down by rule and custom, must follow the beaten track. This hand, on the contrary, though submitting everything to scientific examination, will not be so influenced by prejudice, but will proceed cautiously and thoroughly to logical conclusions, and will find its vocation in a scientific career, or in one involving logic and reason.

THE SQUARE HAND WITH KNOTTY FINGERS

This type is generally found with long fingers, and gives, in the first place, extreme love of detail. It is also fond of construction; it builds plans from any *given* point to any *known* possibility; it may not produce great inventors, but it will produce good architects, mathematicians, and calculators, and if it applies itself to medical work, or to science of any kind, it will choose some speciality and use its love of detail in the perfection of its own particular study.

THE SQUARE HAND WITH SPATULATE FINGERS

This is the hand of invention, but always on practical lines. Men with this formation run the gamut in invention, but on a

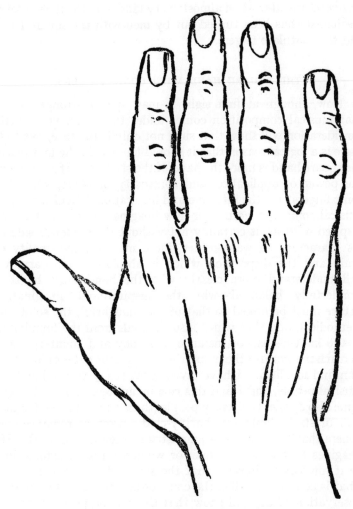

THE SQUARE, OR USEFUL HAND

Fig. 2

practical plane. They make useful things, instruments, and household articles, and are, as well, good engineers. They love mechanical work of almost every kind, and the finest useful mechanism has been turned out by men with the square hand and the spatulate fingers.

THE SQUARE HAND WITH CONIC FINGERS

Now, though at first sight it may appear strange to say that musical composition comes under this head, yet a little consideration will show that such not only is the case, but that there is a logical reason that it should be so. In the first place, the square hand is more the hand of the student. It gives more the power of application and continuity of effort, while the conic fingers give the intuitive and inspirational faculties. The musical composer, no matter how imaginative, no matter how inspired in ideas, is certainly not without the student's side to his character. If we consider, for a moment, the quality of brain and the disposition which is absolutely necessary, we will understand more clearly why the hand must be thus wonderfully balanced—why the inspirational, imaginative nature must be linked to that of the thoughtful, the solid, the methodical, and that which also proceeds from the foundation of the known—as, for instance, harmony and counterpoint— to reach the world of the unknown, through the gates of imagination and idealism. I have given great study to the hands of musical people, and I find this rule invariable. I find that the same also applies to literary people, those who from the foundation of study build up the ivy-clad towers of romance. It is here that the student of palmistry is often discouraged. He imagines that because a man or woman leads an artistic life, be it musical or literary, that the shape of the hand must be what is commonly called the conic or artistic; but the smallest observation of life will show that though the people with the purely conic or artistic hands have the artistic nature and the appreciation of what is artistic, yet they may not have—and I have more often observed that they have not—the power or the ability to bring their ideas before the world in the same masterful way in which the mixed square and conic do. A man of a very artistic spirit, with the conic hand, once said to me: "It is sufficient for the artist to be the artist to his own inner nature; the approbation of the world is, after all, only the vulgar hall-mark on what he knows is gold." "Yes," I reply, "sufficient for your own nature, perhaps, but not sufficient for the world that expects the diamond to shine and the gold to glitter. If the flower made itself, then might it refuse to allow its perfume to scent the earth." On the contrary, the square type will exert its powers to the greatest advantage of all mankind.

THE SQUARE HAND AND PSYCHIC FINGERS

The square hand with purely psychic fingers is rarely found, but an approach to it is often seen in the form of the square palm combined with long, pointed fingers and long nails. Such a formation causes people to start well, and mean well, but makes them subservient to every mood and caprice. An artist with such a type will have a studio of unfinished pictures, and the business man will have his office filled with unfinished plans. Such a blending of types the extreme opposite of each other makes a nature too contradictory ever to succeed.

THE SQUARE HAND AND MIXED FINGERS

This is a type that is very often seen, and more so among men than among women. It consists of every finger being different in shape, sometimes two or three, sometimes all. It is often found that the thumb of such a hand is supple, or bends back very much in the middle joint; the first finger is generally pointed, the second square, the third spatulate, and the fourth pointed. Such a hand indicates great versatility of ideas; at times such a man will be full of inspiration, again he will be scientific and extremely logical; he will descend from the most imaginative idea to the most practical; he will discuss any subject with the greatest ease; but from want of continuity of purpose, he will rarely, if ever, rise to any great height of power or success.

I have not space at my disposal to give the subdivisions of every type, but this is an example for the student of how the seven types may be divided.

CHAPTER IV

THE SPATULATE HAND

THE spatulate hand is so called not only because the tip of each finger resembles the spatula which chemists use in mortars, but also because the palm, instead of having the squareness of the preceding type, is either unusually broad at the wrist or at the base of the fingers (Fig. 3).

When the greater breadth of formation is at the wrist, the palm of the hand becomes pointed toward the fingers; when, on the contrary, the greatest breadth is found at the base of the fingers, the shape of the hand slopes back toward the wrist. We will discuss these two points a little later, but we must first consider the significance of the spatulate hand itself.

In the first place, the spatulate hand, when hard and firm, indicates a nature restless and excitable, but full of energy of purpose and enthusiasm. When soft and flabby, which is often the case, it denotes the restless but irritable spirit. Such a person works in fits and starts, but cannot stick to anything long. Now, in the first place, the peculiar attribute that the spatulate hand has is its intense love of action, energy, and independence. It belongs to the great navigators, explorers, discoverers, and also the great engineers and mechanics, but it is by no means confined to such people, and may be found in almost every walk of life. As a rule, it is a large hand, with fairly long, well-developed fingers. The most striking characteristic of all is the singular independence of spirit that characterizes individuals possessing such a development. It is doubtless this spirit that makes them explorers and discoverers, and causes them also to depart from the known rules of engineering and mechanics to seek the unknown, and thus become famous for their inventions. No matter in what grade or position in life these spatulate hands find themselves, they always in some form strike out for themselves, and assert their right to possess a marked individuality of their own. A singer,

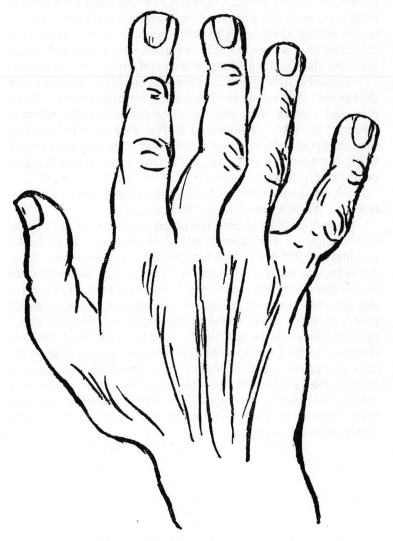

THE SPATULATE, OR ACTIVE HAND

Fig. 3

actress, doctor, or preacher with such a development will break all rules of precedent—not by any means for the sake of eccentricity, but simply because they have an original way of looking at things, and their sense of independence inclines them to resent suiting their brain to other people's ideas. It is from this hand that we get not only our great discoverers and engineers, but also the whole army of men and women we are pleased to call cranks, simply because they will not follow the rut made by the centuries of sheep that have gone before them. Such men and women with the spatulate hands are the advance agents of thought. They are, it is true, very often before their time; they are often wrong in the way they set about their work; but they are, as a rule, the heralds of some new thought or life that will, years later, give life to their fellow men.

This brings us down to the two divisions I have just mentioned. We will now consider their meaning.

The spatulate hand with the broad development at the base of the fingers is the more practical of the two. If he be an inventor, he will use his talents for making locomotives, ships, railways, and all the more useful things of life, for the simple reason that he comes nearer the formation of the square type. But if he has the greater angular development at the wrist, his bent will be for action in the domain of ideas. He will invent flying-machines if he has the inventive talent, hunt for new flowers if he be a botanist, be the demigod of some new gospel if he be a priest. These people wonder that God took six days to make the earth—with the little power that they possess they would revolutionize the world in a day. But they all have their purpose in the evolution of life; they are necessary, therefore they are created.

CHAPTER V

THE PHILOSOPHIC HAND

THE name of this type explains itself, the word "philosophic" being derived from the Greek *philos*, love, and *sophia*, wisdom. This shape of hand is easily recognized: it is generally long and angular, with bony fingers, developed joints, and long nails (Fig. 4). As far as success in the form of wealth is concerned, it is not a favourable type to have; it gleans wisdom, rarely, if ever, gold. People with such a type are, as a rule, students, but of peculiar subjects. They study mankind; they know every chord and tone in the harp of life; they play upon it, and are gratified with its responsive melody more than with the clink of coin. In this way they have as much ambition as other types of humanity, only theirs is of a different kind, that is all. They like to be distinct from other people, and they will go through all kinds of privations to attain this end; but as knowledge gives power, so does the knowledge of mankind give power over man. Such people love mystery in all things. If they preach, they preach over the heads of the people; if they paint, they are mystic; if they are poets, they discard the dramatic clash and colour of life for the visionary similes and vapourish drapings of the spirit. Theirs is the peace of the æsthetic; theirs the domain beyond the borderland of matter; theirs the cloudland of thought, where the dreaded grub-worm of materialism dare not follow. Such hands are found very largely among the Oriental nations, particularly in India. The Brahmans, Yogis, and other mystics possess them in great numbers. In England, striking examples are found in the hands of Cardinal Newman, Cardinal Manning, and Tennyson. They are also largely seen among the Jesuits of the Catholic Church, rarely in the English Church, and more rarely still in Baptists, Presbyterians, and Independents. In character they are silent and secretive; they are deep thinkers, careful over little matters, even in the use of little words; they are proud

55

with the pride of being different from others; they rarely forget an injury, but they are patient with the patience of power. They wait for opportunities, and so opportunities serve them. Such hands are generally egotistical, which is in keeping with the life they lead.   When in any excess of development they are more or less fanatical in religion or mysticism.   Of this the most wonderful examples are found in the East, where from the earliest childhood the Yogi will separate himself from all claims of relationship and kindred, and starve and kill the body that the soul may live.   I differ in my definition of this type very largely from other writers on palmistry.   I fear it has been too often the case that the writer on this subject has followed too closely what other authorities have said, without taking the trouble to follow out his own observations.   The greatest injury that has been done to palmistry has been done in the nineteenth century, by the "lady and gentleman" writers of the day.   Such people read a few books, devote sometimes a few months, sometimes less, to the study as a fad, or as something by which to make a tinsel reputation of being interesting, then they write their names to a book and disappear into the whirl of society from whence they came.   I recall reading a pamphlet written by a lady who eight months earlier had not known a line on the hand, but with astonishing temerity she launched out as an exponent of palmistry, and, having mixed up the types in her brain, wrote that the square hand with short fingers was the hand of poetry and idealism.   In this work I have endeavoured to keep an unbiased mind toward the difference of opinion on this or that in connection with the study.   When I have come in contact with an opinion in opposition to my own, I have carefully considered all points for and against, and before deciding in any direction I have taken time to examine often hundreds of hands before coming to a conclusion on even the smallest point.   When one considers the opportunities placed at my disposal, not only in one country, but in almost every country in the world, he will more readily understand that there is some likelihood of my being, not infallible, but fairly accurate.

With these hands, therefore, it must be borne in mind that the developed joints are the peculiar characteristic of thoughtful people, while the smooth, pointed fingers are the reverse.

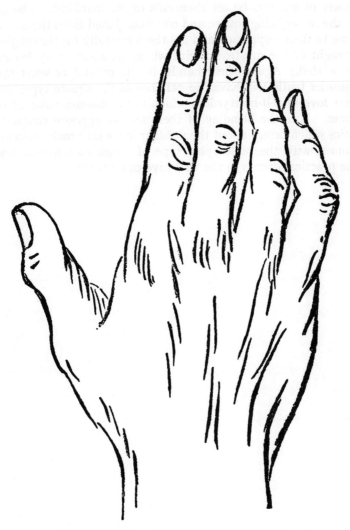

THE KNOTTY, OR PHILOSOPHIC HAND

Fig. 4

Again, such a development gives the love of analysing, but it is the shape or type of hand which determines whether that power of analysis be for chemicals or for mankind. The end of the finger being square and conic combined gives the solemn tone to their inspiration and fits them specially for the religious thought or the mysticism with which, as a rule, they become associated. Again, these hands, in the pursuit of what they consider truth, will have the patience of the square type, with that love of self-martyrdom which is the characteristic of the conic. It is the blending of these almost opposite characteristics which brings about the peculiar ideas that make men and women with the philosophic type of hands so different from the practical drones in the vast hive of humanity.

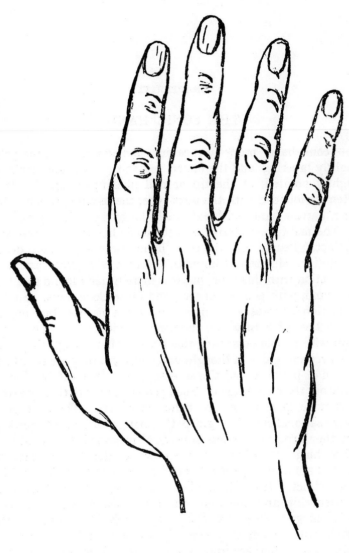

THE CONIC, OR ARTISTIC HAND

Fig. 5

CHAPTER VI

THE CONIC HAND

THE conic hand, properly speaking, is medium-sized, the palm slightly tapering, and the fingers full at the base, and conic, or slightly pointed, at the tip or nail phalange (Fig. 5). It is often confounded with the next type, the psychic, which is the long, narrow hand, with extremely long, tapering fingers.

The main characteristics of the conic hand are impulse and instinct. People with the conic hand are often, in fact, designated "the children of impulse." There is a great variety in connection with this type, but it is more usually found as a full, soft hand, with pointed fingers, and rather long nails. Such a formation denotes an artistic, impulsive nature, but one in which love of luxury and indolence predominate. The great fault with people possessing this type is, that though they may be clever and quick in thought and ideas, yet they are so utterly devoid of patience and tire so easily, that they rarely, if ever, carry out their intentions. Such people appear to their greatest advantage in company, or before strangers. They are good conversationalists, they grasp the drift of a subject quickly, but they are more or less superficial in knowledge, as also in other things; they have not the power of the student, through want of application; they do not reason, they judge by impulse and instinct. It is that quality which makes them changeable in friendship and affection; one can easily offend them over little things. They are also very much influenced by the people with whom they come in contact, and by their surroundings. They are impressionable in *affaires de cœur*; they carry their likes and dislikes to extremes; they are usually quick-tempered, but temper with them is but a thing of the moment. They, however, when out of temper, speak their mind plainly, and are too impetuous to study words or expressions. They are always generous and sympathetic, selfish where their own personal comfort is concerned, it is true, but not in money matters; they are easily influenced to give money for charity, but, alas! here they have not the power of discrimination, consequently the money is given to anybody or anything which may rouse their sympathies at the moment. These hands never get that credit for charity which falls to the lot of the more practical types. To get credit for charity very often consists in saving what we give to the beggar and giving it to the church, but the conic fingers never think of that. The beggar comes, and if the impulse to give is there—well, they give, and that is all.

This interesting type has been called, and deservedly so, the artistic, but such relates more to temperament than to the carrying out of the artistic ideas. It would really be more correct to say that the owners of such hands are influenced by the artistic, than that they are artistic. They are more easily influenced by colour, music, eloquence, tears, joy, or sorrow, than any other type. Men and women possessing this class of hand respond quickly to sympathetic influences; they are emotional, and rise to the greatest heights of rapture, or descend to the lowest depths of despair, over any trifle.

When the conic hand is hard and elastic, it denotes all the good qualities of the first-mentioned, but accentuated by greater energy and firmness of will. The hard conic hand is artistic in nature, and if encouraged for an artistic life the energy and determination will go far toward making success. It will have all the quickness of the first, with all the brilliancy and sparkle in company and before strangers, and it is for that reason that the conic hand has been chosen to represent those who lead a public life, such as actors, actresses, singers, orators, and all those who follow a purely emotional career. But it must not be forgotten that such people depend more upon the inspirational feeling of the moment than thought, reason, or study. They will do things well, but will not know why or how they do them. The singer will carry away her audience by her own individuality more than by study of the song; the actress, from her own emotional nature, will stir the emotions of others; and the orator will move multitudes by the eloquence of his tongue—not by the logic of his words. It must, therefore, be remembered that the type of hand but relates to the natural temperament and disposition of the individual; it is the foundation upon which the talent rises or falls. For instance, a woman with square fingers can be as great a singer, and may often be capable of rising to greater things than the woman with the pointed formation; but she will reach that point by different means—by her application, by her study, by her conscientious work, and by the greater power of endurance and patience that she possesses. Study and development are one half the ladder of fame. Genius sits on the rungs to dream, Study works and rises rung by rung; it is the earthworms alone who, dazzled by the heights above them, confound the two, and oft crown Study and call it Genius. The artistic type as a type but relates to temperament; the variety of fingers indicates only where that temperament is strongest: as, for instance, the artistic hand with square fingers indicates more the student, and, consequently, more exactness in foundation, method, and correctness; such persons will try and try again until they are successful.

The spatulate fingers on the artistic hand will give, say, to a painter the greater breadth of design and colour, the more daring ideas that will make the man famous for his originality. The philosophic will give the mystical treatment of the idea— the tones and semitones that subdue the already subdued colours. The lights and shades that creep across the canvas, the poem in the petals of the asphodel, the *Benedictus* in the hands that soothe the dying—all will be detail, but detail leading to the regions of the spirit; all will be calm, but with that calmness that awes one with the sense of the mysterious.

CHAPTER VII

THE PSYCHIC HAND

THE most beautiful but the most unfortunate of the seven is
what is known as the psychic (Fig. 6). This in its purity of
type is a very rare hand to find. The name explains itself—
that which appertains to the soul. The very word seems to
suggest to one's mind the old fable of the envy of Venus toward
the maiden Psyche—the war of the goddess of passion against
the more spiritual charm of the daughter of the soul. In its
pureness of type it is a hard hand to find: our contemporary
civilization does not encourage such rare flowers of lily whiteness
and icy purity; the calmness, coldness, and dreamy chastity
of such a type are not sought after by the present-day sons of
the soil, whose heads are bowed in the quest for gold, and whose
blood is heated by the closeness of the cattle. But although the
exact type may be hard to find, yet there are hundreds of men
and women who so approach the psychic that they must be
considered part of it, particularly when the customs that control our present-day life are taken into consideration. The
psychic is the most beautiful hand of all. It is in formation
long, narrow, and fragile-looking, with slender, tapering fingers
and long, almond-shaped nails. Its very fineness and beauty,
however, indicate its want of energy and strength, and one
instinctively pities such hands if they have to try to hold their
own in the battle of life.

Individuals with the psychic hand have the purely visionary,
idealistic nature. They appreciate the beautiful in every shape
and form; they are gentle in manner, quiet in temper; they
are confiding, and they instinctively trust every one who is kind
to them. They have no idea of how to be practical, business-
like, or logical; they have no conception of order, punctuality,
or discipline; they are easily influenced by others; against their
will, they are carried away by the strong rush of humanity.
Colour appeals to this nature in the highest possible way; to

some, every tone of music, every joy, every sorrow, every emotion is reflected in a colour. This type is unconsciously a religious one; it feels what is true, but has not the power to seek truth. In religion such people will be more impressed with the service, the music, and the ceremony than with the logic or truth of the sermon. They are innately devotional, they seem to dwell on the confines of the spiritual, they feel the awe and the mystery of life, without knowing why. All forms of magic and mystery attract them; they are easily imposed upon, and yet bitterly resent being deceived. These individuals have the intuitive faculties highly developed; they are good as sensitives, mediums, clairvoyants, because they are more alive to feelings, instincts, and impressions than are their more matter-of-fact brothers and sisters.

Parents having such children generally do not at all understand how to treat them. The strange thing is that they are often the offspring of matter-of-fact, practical people. The only way in which I would account for such a fact is by the theory of balance: nature, working through hereditary laws, finds a point of balance by producing the direct opposite of the parent; thus the law of reaction produces the type under examination. Alas! too often a temperament of this kind, by the ignorance and stupidity of the parents, is forced into some business life, simply because the father is in business. The utter wrongness of the life so crushes and dwarfs the nature that very often the result of such environment is insanity or an early grave. There is no question but that the asylums of the world are largely filled by the utter inability of parents for such a position of responsibility; and the sooner this fact is recognized, the better.

Possessors of these beautiful, delicate hands, the indicators of the purely sensitive nature, usually feel their position in life so keenly that they too often consider themselves useless, and become morbid and melancholy in consequence. Such, however, is not the case; there is nothing useless that nature calls into creation; the beauty and sweetness of such temperaments are often of more use and do more good than those who, by the accumulation of this world's goods, build a convent or endow a church. They may be placed here to establish a balance in the laws of humanity; they may be here to increase our love

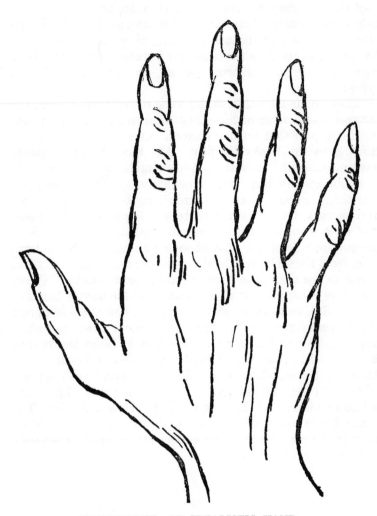

THE PSYCHIC, OR IDEALISTIC HAND

Fig. 6

and appreciation of the beautiful; but they are not useless —of that we may be assured; therefore let us encourage and help them, instead of crushing and destroying them as we too often do. Alas! in the worldly sense they are generally left far behind in the race for fame and fortune. I cannot refrain from drawing the following picture, as illustrative of such types:

They are as lilies thrown, by some ruthless hand, upon the tempest-tossed river of life—they seem so helpless in the onward sweep of that terrible current. One sees them at times clinging to the banks for pity. Ah! those beautiful hands have no strength; they are swept on again by the rising tide of bubbling, babbling, frothy humanity. A little lower, one sees them, soiled and stained, crouching beneath the shadow of some rock, trying, as it were, to look happy amid the weeds that for a moment mock the stream. Again, it is the rush of the onward tide or the wash of some passing barge that drags them from the shelter of the stone and hurries them nearer and nearer to the sea. The river is broader now, quieter, calmer, wider; we expand in our views as we leave the narrow banks of youth. See, now, as the night is nearing, how those lilies rest and dream upon the tide. The river is silent now, the rush is past, the day of life is done. See how it bears the broken flowers tenderly, as if sorry for the roughness of its early tide. All is quiet now, all is calm. Wider and wider yet it grows, calmer and yet still calmer. The end has come. The mists fall now, thicker and closer and whiter. How still it is! The silence hangs like a coldness on the heart. The river widens out into the sea, and lilies and flowers and weeds drift—it may be to the garden of God.

CHAPTER VIII

THE MIXED HAND

THE mixed hand is the most difficult of all to describe. In the chapter on the square hand I gave an illustration of that type with mixed fingers. In that case, however, the mixed fingers have the foundation of the square hand, whereas with the true mixed type no such foundation can be cited for the student's guidance.

The mixed type is so called because the hand cannot possibly be classed as square, spatulate, conic, philosophic, or psychic; the fingers also belong to different types—often one pointed, one square, one spatulate, one philosophic, etc.

The mixed hand is the hand of ideas, of versatility, and generally of changeability of purpose. A man with such a hand is adaptable to both people and circumstances, clever, but erratic in the application of his talents. He will be brilliant in conversation, be the subject science, art, or gossip. He may play some instrument fairly well, may paint a little, and so on; but rarely will he be great. When, however, a strong line of head rules the hand, he will, of all his talents, choose the best, and add to it the brilliancy and versatility of the others. Such hands find their greatest scope in work requiring diplomacy and tact. They are so versatile that they have no difficulty in getting on with the different dispositions with which they come into contact. Their most striking peculiarity is their adaptibility to circumstances: they never feel the ups and downs of fortune like others; almost all classes of work are easy to them. They are generally inventive, particularly if they can thereby relieve themselves of labour. They are restless and do not remain long in any town or place. They are fond of new ideas: one moment they determine to write a drama, the next, perhaps, they invent a gas-stove or go into politics; but as they are always changing, and unstable as water, they rarely succeed. It must be remembered that when the palm

belongs to a certain type these characteristics are much modified; as, for instance, mixed fingers on the square, the spatulate,
the philosophic, or the conic will often succeed where the pure
development of the type would fail.   When the entire hand is
mixed it is then that, through versatility of talent and purpose,
the subject is inclined to become the "Jack of all trades," to
which class of unfortunates the individual possessing this type
of hand is so commonly relegated in works on palmistry.

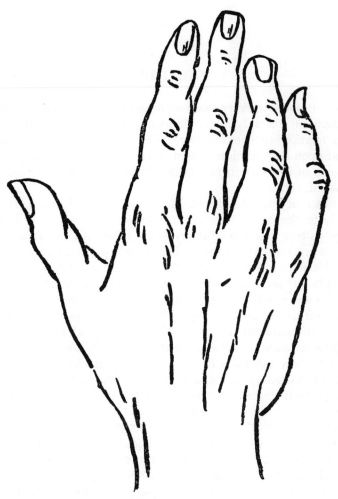

THE MIXED HAND

Fig. 7

CHAPTER IX

THE THUMB

THE thumb is in every sense so important that it calls for special attention, not only in the domain of cheirognomy, but also in its relation to cheiromancy. The truth of palmistry could rest upon the solid foundation given by the study of the thumb alone, in its relation to the most important characteristics of the subject.

In every age the thumb has played a conspicuous part, not only in the hand, but also in the world itself. It is a well-known fact that among many of the tribes of Oriental nations, if the prisoner, when brought before his captors, cover his thumb by his fingers, he is in this dumb but eloquent fashion giving up his will and independence, and begging for mercy. We find in the war annals of the children of Israel instances of their cutting off the thumbs of their enemies. Gipsies, in their judgment of character, make the thumb the great foundation for all their remarks. Being interested with gipsies in my early life, I know this for a fact, for I have seen and watched them from the position, angle, and general appearance of the thumb make their calculations accordingly. In India they have a variety of systems by which they read the hand, but here, again, they make the thumb the centre and foundation, no matter what system they work out. The Chinese also believe in palmistry, and they, too, base their remarks on the position of the thumb itself. Again, it is an interesting fact to notice that even in Christianity the thumb has played an important role, the thumb representing God; the first finger Christ, the indicator of the will of God, and the only finger on the hand that has by virtue of its position, the power to point, or to stand upright independent of the rest; the second representing the Holy Ghost, as the attendant to the first. In the Greek Church the bishop alone gives the blessing by the thumb and first and second fingers, representing the Trinity; the ordinary priest has to use the whole hand. And, again, in the old ritual of the English Church, we find that in baptism the cross must be made by the thumb.

I do not wish to tire my readers by going into a lengthy dissertation upon the medical points which could be given by the hundred in proof of the importance of this member; but the most significant of all is that which relates to what is known in medical work as the "thumb centre" of the brain. It is a well-known fact among the specialists of nerve diseases that by an examination of the thumb they can tell if the patient is affected or is likely to be affected by paralysis or not, as the thumb will indicate such a likelihood a long time before there has appeared the slightest trace of such a disease in any other part of the system. If it indicate such an affection, an operation is at once performed on the thumb centre of the brain, and if that operation is successful (which is again shown by the thumb) they have baffled the disease and the patient is saved. And yet, in face of this, which is a well-known fact, there still are people who do not believe in the study of the hand. Dr. Francis Galton once demonstrated in London the marvellous accuracy by which criminals can be traced by the study of the corrugations of the skin of the thumb. *En passant*, the English government thought well of the idea, and even proposed to put it into practice—and yet that very government arrested and prosecuted palmists during the same year in almost every part of the country. Justice is indeed blind. Another very interesting point is the old idea of the midwives—an idea, by the way, that can easily be seen to contain a good deal of truth. They believed that if the child, some days after birth, was inclined to keep the thumb inside the fingers, it foreshadowed great physical delicacy, but if, seven days after birth, the thumb was still covered, then there was good reason to suspect that the child would be delicate mentally. If one will visit the asylums of the country, he cannot fail to notice that all congenital idiots have very weak, poor thumbs; in fact, some are so weak as not to be properly developed, even in shape. All weak-minded individuals have weak thumbs, and the man or woman who will stand talking with the fingers covering and concealing the thumb has little self-confidence or self-reliance. It is an interesting thing to watch the hands of people when dying.

One will see that, as death approaches and the reason goes, the thumb loses all power and drops in on the hand, but that if the reason has only faded temporarily the thumb still retains its power and there is every hope of life. It is D'Arpentigny who has said, "The thumb individualizes the man." This is remarkably true, particularly when one follows out Sir Charles Bell's discovery that in the hand of the chimpanzee, which is the nearest approach to the human, though well formed in every way, yet the thumb, if measured, does not reach the base of the first finger. The deduction to be made is, therefore, that the higher and better-proportioned the thumb, the more the intellectual faculties rule, and vice versa. This point the student will prove by the most casual observation. The man with the short, clumsy, thick-set thumb is coarse and brutish in his ideas and animal in his instincts, while the man or woman with the long, well-shaped thumb is intellectual and refined, and in the attainment of a desire, or the carrying out of an object, such a person will use the strength of intellectual will, as opposed to that of brute force, which will be applied by the man with the thick, short formation. The thumb, therefore, should be long and firm upon the hand. It should not stand at right angles to the palm, nor yet should it lie too close to the side. It should have a slope toward the fingers, and yet not lie down on them. When it stands off the hand, at right angles to it, the nature will fly to extremes, from sheer independence of spirit. It will be impossible to manage or control such natures; they will brook no opposition, and they will be inclined to the aggressive in their manner and bearing. When the thumb is well formed, but lying down, cramped toward the fingers, it indicates the utter want of independence of spirit. It denotes a nervous, timorous, but cautious nature; it will be impossible to find out what such a person is thinking about or what he intends to do; he cannot be outspoken, because his nature is the reverse. If the thumb, however, is a long one, he will use his intellectual faculties to outwit his opponent, but if it be short and thick he will cautiously await his opportunity for any deed of violence that he may meditate. When a well-formed thumb, therefore, strikes the happy medium of these two extremes, the subject will have sufficient independence of spirit to give him dignity and force of character; he will also be properly cautious over his own affairs, and have strength of will and decision. It therefore stands: the long, well-formed thumb denotes strength of intellectual will; the short, thick thumb, brute force and obstinacy; the small, weak thumb, weakness of will and want of energy.

From time immemorial the thumb has been divided into three parts, which are significant of the three great powers that rule the world—love, logic, and will.

The first or nail phalange denotes will.

The second phalange, logic.

The third, which is the boundary of the Mount of Venus, love.

When the thumb is unequally developed, as, for instance, the first phalange extremely long, we find that the subject depends upon neither logic nor reason, but simply upon will.

When the second phalange is much longer than the first, the subject, though having all the calmness and exactitude of reason, yet has not sufficient will and determination to carry out his ideas.

When the third phalange is long and the thumb small, the man or woman is a prey to the more passionate or sensual side of the nature.

One of the most interesting things in the study of the thumb is to notice whether the first joint is supple or stiff. When supple, the first phalange is allowed to bend back, and forms the thumb into an arch; when, on the contrary, the thumb is stiff, the first phalange cannot be bent back, even by pressure; and these two opposite peculiarities bear the greatest possible relation to character.

The supple thumb (Fig. 8) is the distinctive peculiarity of the Latin races; the stiff joint is more the property of the Northern. The supple joint, for instance, is very rare among the Danes, Norwegians, Germans, English, and Scotch, whereas it is found in large numbers among the Irish, French, Spanish, Italians, and wherever these races have congregated. I hardly think that the theory of climatic influence bears out this point. I am more inclined to consider that the unconscious influence of the surroundings, prenatal or otherwise, has more to do with this peculiarity, for the characteristics that it shows in the individual are also the characteristics of the nation to which that individual belongs.

THE SUPPLE-JOINTED THUMB

For example, the supple-jointed thumb, bending from the hand, is the indication of the extravagant person, not only in matters of money, but in thought; these are life's natural spendthrifts—improvident of time, improvident of wealth. They have adaptability of temperament for both people and circumstances; they are quickly at home in whatever society they are thrown; they have the sentimental love of kindred and country, as opposed to the practical; they settle down easily to new work and new surroundings, and consequently they quickly make a home in whatever country they are placed.

THE FIRM-JOINTED THUMB

Again, in a general way, the exact opposite of all this is found among the people with the stiff, firm joint (Fig. 8). In the first place, they are more practical; they have a strong will and a kind of stubborn determination which makes them rather stronger in character, and which is a large element in their success. They are more cautious and secretive; they advance by slow steps where the other nature will act by leaps and bounds. Again, they are not erratic like the first-mentioned; they stick to one thing; they carry out their purpose with a kind of resistless stubbornness; they have the practical idea of making the most out of their own home and their own country; they rule with strength; they have a keen sense of justice; they control self as they would control machinery; in war they are solid, strong, and resistless; in love they are undemonstrative, but firm and staunch; in religion their churches are plain, but solid; in art they have the strength of their own individuality.

THE SECOND PHALANGE

The next important characteristic of the thumb is the shape and make of the second or middle phalange. It will be found

(a) The Clubbed Thumb

(b) Supple-jointed Thumb.   (c) Firm-jointed Thumb

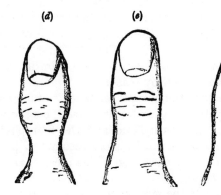

(d)   (e)   (f)

THE THUMBS

Fig. 8

that this varies greatly and is a decided indicator of temperament. It has two noticeable formations, namely, the narrow moulded centre or waist-like appearance (Fig. 8, *d*), and its opposite, which is full and more clumsy (Fig. 8, *f*).

When I published my *Book on the Hand*, which was to be followed later by this larger and fuller work, I called attention to the great difference, as far as character is concerned, shewn by these two formations. My statement that the waist-like appearance indicated tact aroused a good deal of interest, and as it was taken exception to by some of my critics, I will here endeavour to show in a logical way why such should be the case. In the first place, the student has by this time seen the truth of my remarks about the finer formation of the thumb being the indication of the greater development of the intellectual will, and the coarse formation that of the nature that will use more brute force in the accomplishment of an object. It therefore follows that the waist-like appearance, which is a portion of the finer development, indicates the tact born of mental power, whereas the fuller, coarser development indicates force in the carrying out of a purpose, in keeping with the characteristics of each nature.

When the first or nail phalange is thick and heavy, with a short, flat nail, it is a sure indication of the ungovernable passion of the subject. All brutal animal natures have such clubbed formations, the force of blind passion completely dominating whatever reason they possess. Such people, as a rule, also have the first joint stiff, and the two points together give that terrible obstinacy of purpose that drives the subject, once out of temper, into deeds of violence and crime. The flat first phalange, consequently, whether short or long, is more calm in matters of temper and more controlled by reason.

When the hand is hard the natural tendency toward energy and firmness indicated by the thumb is increased; consequently the subject with the hard, firm hand and the first phalange of the thumb well developed will be more resolute of purpose and more determined in the execution of his ideas than is the subject with the soft hand.

When the hand is soft the subject will be more inclined to use his will by fits and starts, but cannot be so much depended upon in the execution of his plans.

One very striking peculiarity to be found in this study of human nature through the medium of the hand is shewn in the case of people with the supple or bending-back thumb. They rarely have the same keenness of moral consciousness that is found with those of the straight, firm development. They are generally more those impulsive children of nature in whom conscience in morals does not play so important a part.

CHAPTER X

THE JOINTS OF THE FINGERS

THE development or non-development of the joints of the fingers is a very important consideration in the reading of the hand. The joints are, figuratively speaking, walls between the phalanges, and are important indications of the peculiarities as well as of the temperament of the subject.

When the subject has what are known as smooth joints he is more inclined to be impulsive in thought and to arrive at conclusions without using the reasoning faculties. With square hands this is very much modified, but not by any means eradicated. Consequently a scientific man with square fingers, but with smooth joints (Fig. 9, *a*), will jump at conclusions without being always able to account for them. Such a doctor will diagnose a patient in the same way; if the man be really talented he may be very accurate in his conclusions, but such a man is more apt to make mistakes than the man with the square type with developed joints. With the pointed hands the smooth joints are purely intuitive (Fig. 9, *b*); they cannot be troubled with details of any kind; they are also careless in dress, appearance, and in little matters. Such a person in business affairs could not keep papers and little things in their places, although he would be very particular in insisting upon order in other people.

The opposite is found in the case of people with the developed joints (Fig. 9, *c*). Work has nothing to do with the increase or diminution of such formations; the smooth joints are as often found among men who do the hardest kind of manual labour as the knotty or developed joints among men who do nothing but mental work. They are sometimes found running in families for generations, or appearing in one child and but slightly found in all the others. In the breeding of animals it may be observed, *en passant*, how often little peculiarities of this kind occur, and also how significant they are. Thus,

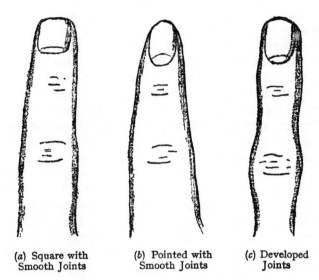

(a) Square with   (b) Pointed with   (c) Developed
    Smooth Joints   Smooth Joints   Joints

THE JOINTS OF THE FINGERS

Fig. 9

when one considers how wonderful are the laws of heredity, he will study these "little things" with greater interest. For instance, there is that well-known fact that if a woman gives birth to a child by her first husband, children who follow by the second, third, or even fourth husband, as the case may be, all in some slight way exhibit the peculiarities of the first husband.

The developed joints being the opposite of the smooth, it follows that they show more exactness in method and work. In this case, a man with the square hand and developed joints, engaged in some scientific pursuit, does not care how much time he spends in working out details in connection with any science in which he is engaged. It is the same reason that makes the philosophic hands so exact about detail in connection with their work. The owners of these joints notice the slightest thing out of place in even the arrangement of a room. They worry over little things, though in important matters they will be cool and calm. Men with these developed joints have an almost feminine instinct in matters of dress—they class and blend colour well, and nothing will irritate them more than to accompany a woman the colours of whose costume do not harmonize. In dramatic work, people with such joints are careful and accurate in the delineation of character, but lack dramatic breadth and force. Outside of science, they perhaps make their best mark in literature, because of their extraordinary power of analysing human nature, and because of the true instinct and knowledge of humanity which seems to come to them without effort. We must therefore draw the deduction that these developed walls or joints between the phalanges, figuratively speaking, stop the tide of impulse, and make the nature more observant, thoughtful and analysing.

CHAPTER XI

THE FINGERS

FINGERS are either long or short, irrespective of the length of the palm to which they belong.

Long fingers give love of detail in everything—in the decoration of a room, in the treatment of servants, in the management of nations, or in the painting of a picture. Long-fingered people are exact in matters of dress, quick to notice small attentions; they worry themselves over little things, and have occasionally a leaning toward affectation.

Short fingers are quick and impulsive. They cannot be troubled about little things; they take everything *en masse*; they generally jump to conclusions too hastily. They do not care so much about appearances, or for the conventionalities of society; they are quick in thought, and hasty and outspoken in speech.

Fingers thick and clumsy, as well as short, are more or less cruel and selfish.

When the fingers are stiff and curved inward, or naturally contracted, they denote an excess of caution and reserve, and very often indicate a cowardly spirit.

When they are very supple and bend back like an arch, they tell of a nature charming in company, affable and clever, but curious and inquisitive.

Naturally crooked, distorted, twisted fingers on a bad hand indicate a crooked, distorted, evil nature; on a good hand they are rarely found, but if found they denote a quizzical, irritating person.

When a small fleshy ball or pad is found on the inside of the nail phalange, it denotes extreme sensitiveness and tact through the dread of causing pain to others.

When the fingers are thick and puffy at the base, the subject considers his own comfort before that of others; he will desire luxury in eating, drinking, and living. When, on the contrary, the fingers at the base are shaped like a waist, it shows an unselfish disposition in every way, and fastidiousness in matters of food.

When, with the fingers open, a wide space is seen between the first and second, it indicates great independence of thought. When the space is wide between the third and fourth, it indicates independence of action.

THE LENGTH OF THE FINGERS IN RELATION TO ONE ANOTHER

The first finger on some hands is very short; again, on others, it is as long as the second, and so on.

When the first, or index finger, is excessively long, it denotes great pride, and a tendency to rule and domineer. It is to be found in the hands of priests as well as politicians. Such a man, literally speaking, will "lay down the law."

When this finger is abnormal, namely, as long as the second, it indicates great pride of disposition, a desire for power, the "one man, one world" creed. Napoleon was a striking example of this rule; on his hand the first finger was abnormal, it being fully equal to the second.

When the second finger (the finger of Saturn) is square and heavy, it shows a deeply thoughtful, almost morbid nature.

When pointed, the reverse—callousness and frivolity.

When the third finger (the finger of the Sun) is nearly of the same length as the first, it denotes ambition for wealth and honour through its artistic leanings, and a great desire for glory. If excessively long, almost equal to the second, it denotes the nature that looks at life in the light of a lottery, one that gambles with all things—money, life, and danger—but one endowed withal with strong artistic instincts and talents.

The spatulate termination for this third finger is an excellent sign for the actor, orator, or preacher. It indicates that his artistic gifts are strengthened by the dramatic or sensational power, the breadth, the colour necessary to appeal to audiences.

When the fourth, or little finger, is well shaped and long, it acts as a kind of balance in the hand to the thumb, and indicates the power of the subject to influence others. When very long —almost reaching to the nail of the third—it shows great power of expression in both writing and speaking, and the owner is more or less the savant and philosopher: one who can converse with ease on any subject; one who interests and commands people by the manner in which he will apply facts and knowledge to the treatment of anything brought under his notice.

CHAPTER XII

THE PALM, AND LARGE AND SMALL HANDS

A THIN, hard, dry palm indicates timidity, and a nervous, worrying, troubled nature.

A very thick palm, full and soft, shows sensuality of disposition.

When the palm is firm and elastic, and in proportion to the fingers, it indicates evenness of mind, energy, and quickness of intellect.

When not very thick, but soft and flabby, it denotes indolence, love of luxury, and a tendency toward sensuality.

A hollow palm has been proved to be an unfortunate sign; such people usually have even more disappointments than fall, as a rule, to the lot of mortals. I have also noticed a peculiarity which has not been mentioned in other works on the subject, namely, that the hollow inclines more to one line or portion of the hand than to another.

If it inclines to the line of life, it promises disappointment and trouble in domestic affairs, and if the rest of the hand denotes ill-health, it is an added sign of delicacy and trouble.

When the hollow comes under the line of fate, it indicates misfortune in business, money, and worldly affairs.

When under the line of heart it tells of disappointment in the closest affections.

I do not hold with other works on the subject, that the fingers must be longer than the palm to show the intellectual nature. The palm of the hand is never, properly speaking, exceeded in length by the fingers. How can we expect this to be the case with the square, spatulate, and philosophic types? The statement that in every case the fingers must be longer than the palm is erroneous and misleading.

LARGE AND SMALL HANDS

It is a thing well worth remarking, that, generally speaking, people with large hands do very fine work and love great detail in work, while those with very small hands go in for large things, and cannot bear detail in employment. I once examined the hands of the diamond setters and engravers engaged in some of the largest goldsmiths' establishments in Bond Street, London, and out of nearly a hundred, I did not find a single exception to this rule. One man—and I have the cast before me now—had extraordinarily large hands, yet he was famed for the fineness and minutiæ of the work which those great hands turned out.

Small hands, on the contrary, prefer to carry out large ideas, and, as a rule, make plans far too large for their power of execution. They love to manage large concerns and govern communities, and, speaking generally, even the writing of small hands is large and bold.

CHAPTER XIII

THE NAILS

PARTICULARLY as regards health, and the diseases likely to affect the subject, the nails will be found to be remarkably sure guides. Medical men in both London and Paris have taken up this study of the nails with great interest. Often a patient does not know, or for the moment forgets, what his parents have suffered or died from; but an examination of the nails will in a few seconds disclose important hereditary traits. I will first treat of the health side of the question, then of the disposition, as shown by this study.

In the first place, the care of the nails does not alter or affect their type in the slightest degree: whether they are broken by work or polished by care, the type remains unchanged. For instance, a mechanic may have long nails, and the gentleman at ease may have very short, broad ones, though he manicure them every morning.

Nails are divided into four distinct classes: long, short, broad, and narrow.

LONG NAILS

Long nails never indicate such great physical strength as the short, broad type. Very long-nailed persons are more liable to suffer from chest and lung trouble, and this is more accentuated if the nails are much curved, both from the top back toward the finger and across the finger (Fig. 10, *g*). This tendency is even more aggravated if the nail is fluted or ribbed (Fig. 10, *j*).

This type of nail, when shorter, indicates throat trouble, such as laryngitis, asthma, and bronchial affections (Fig. 10).

Long nails, very wide at the top and bluish in appearance, denote bad circulation proceeding from ill-health, or nervous

86

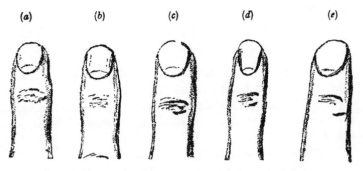

(a)   (b)   (c)   (d)   (e)

Throat Affections.   Bronchial.   Bronchial.

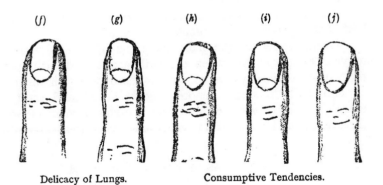

(f)   (g)   (h)   (i)   (j)

Delicacy of Lungs.   Consumptive Tendencies.

NAILS

Fig. 10

prostration. This is very often the case with the hands of women between the ages of fourteen and twenty-one and forty-two and forty-seven.

SHORT NAILS

Short, small nails run in whole families in which there is a tendency toward heart disease (Fig. 11).

Short nails, thin and flat at the base, with little or no moons, are sure signs of weak action of the heart, and, generally speaking, heart disease.

Large moons indicate good circulation.

Short nails, very flat and sunken, as it were, into the flesh at the base, show nerve diseases (Fig. 11).

Short nails, very flat and inclined to curve out or lift up at the edges, are the forerunners of paralysis, particularly if they are white and brittle as well as flat. If the latter is the case the disease is more advanced (Fig. 11, *i*).

Short-nailed people have a greater tendency to suffer from heart trouble and from diseases affecting the trunk and lower limbs than those with long nails.

Long-nailed persons are more liable to trouble in the upper half of the system—in the lungs, chest, and head.

Natural spots on the nails are signs of a highly-strung nervous temperament; when the nails are flecked with spots the whole nervous system requires a thorough overhauling.

Thin nails, if small, denote delicate health and want of energy. Nails very narrow and long, if high and much curved, threaten spinal trouble, and never promise very great strength.

DISPOSITION AS SHOWN BY THE NAILS

In disposition, long-nailed individuals are less critical and more impressionable than those with short nails. They are also calmer in temper and more gentle.

Long nails show more resignation and calmness in every way. As a rule their owners take things easily. Such nails indicate great ideality; they also show an artistic nature, and their owners, as a rule, are fond of poetry, painting, and all the fine arts. Long-nailed persons, however, are rather

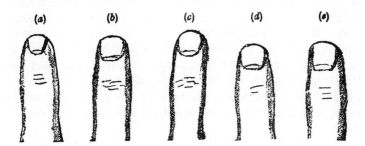

(a) (b) (c) (d) (e)

Showing Bad Circulation and Tendency Towards Heart Disease

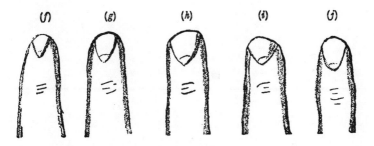

(f) (g) (h) (i) (j)

Showing Tendency Towards Paralysis

NAILS

Fig. 11

inclined to be visionary, and shrink from looking facts in the face, particularly if those facts are distasteful.

Short-nailed individuals, on the contrary, are extemely critical, even of things relating to self; they analyse everything with which they come into contact; they incline to logic, reason, and facts, in opposition to the visionary qualities of the long-nailed. Short-nailed individuals make the best critics; they are quicker, sharper and keener in their judgment; they are, as well, fond of debate, and in an argument they will hold out till the very last; they have a keener sense of humour and of the ridiculous than the long-nailed; they are quick and sharp in temper, and are more or less sceptical of things they do not understand.

When the nails are broader than they are long, they indicate a pugnacious disposition, also a tendency to worry and meddle and to interfere with other people's business.

Nails short by the habit of biting indicate the nervous, worrying temperament.

I do not pay any attention to the spots on the nails, except as a sign of illness through nervous strain.

CHAPTER XIV

THE HAIR ON THE HANDS

A Suggested Theory

IF the exponent of palmistry has to read hands through a curtain, without seeing his subject, the hair growing on the hand, although seemingly unimportant, to a thorough student becomes a study of very great note and magnitude. A slight knowledge of the laws that govern the growth of hair will not, therefore, be out of place. The hair is used by nature to fulfil a great many useful purposes in connection with the body. I will give those only that are necessary to the student of this particular study, namely, the cause of the colour of the hair, of its coarseness and fineness, as illustrative of disposition.

In the first place, each hair is in itself a fine tube; these tubes are in connection with the skin and the skin nerves. These hairs or tubes are, literally speaking, escape-valves for the electricity of the body, and by the colour they take in the passage of that electricity, so should the student be able to determine certain qualities of temperament of which he would otherwise be ignorant. For example: If there is a large amount of iron or pigment in the system, the flow of this electricity through the hair forces it into these tubes and makes the hair black, brown, blond, grey, or white, as the case may be. Individuals with blond or fair hair, therefore, have less iron and dark pigment in the system. As a rule they are more languid, listless, gentle, and more influenced by people and surroundings than those of the darker type.

People with very dark hair, although often less energetic in work, will have more passion in temper, will be more irritable and more energetic in affection than those of the fairer type, and so in every degree of shade until we come to the extreme opposite of the dark type, namely, those with red hair. If we will examine hair, we will find that red hair is coarser in quality as a rule than either black, brown, or blond. Now, being coarser or larger, the tube itself is, consequently, wider, and therefore shows the greater quantity of electricity that escapes, and of which these natures have the greatest amount. It is not that they have as much pigment as the dark people, but having the greater supply and force of electricity, they are consequently the more excitable and quicker to rouse to action than either the black, brown, or blond.

When the system gets old, or becomes enfeebled by excess or dissipation, the electricity, not being generated in such large quantities, is nearly or entirely consumed by the system itself; the pigment is no longer forced into these hair tubes, and consequently they commence to grow white at the outer ends, and so on, till the entire hair or tube becomes white. It is the same in the case of a sudden shock or grief—the hair often stands on end from the force of the nervous electric fluid rushing through these tubes; reaction naturally sets in immediately, and the hair often becomes white in a few hours. Very rarely can the system recover from such a strain, and consequently very rarely will the hair resume its colour.

In America more people are to be found with white hair than, I think, in any other country in the world. It has been suggested that this fact may be due to the high pressure at which many Americans live. The climate of the country has, I consider, a great deal to do with their temperament; the brightness and brilliance of the atmosphere, even in winter, the peculiar nerve-stimulating quality of the air, all combine to cause its men and women to press forward, with a keen spirit of competition, both in work and in amusement. This theory of the colour of the hair has never, to my knowledge, been put forward in this way before. I commend it to the attention of those who do not lose sight of the fact that in the Book of Nature nothing is so small that it may not give us knowledge, and as knowledge is power, let us therefore not be ashamed to seek it, even in little things.

CHAPTER XV

THE MOUNTS, THEIR POSITION AND THEIR MEANINGS

IN my work I always class the mounts of the hand (Fig. 12) with the hand itself, and therefore I treat of them in the section of this work devoted to cheirognomy. Again, in the consideration of this point, I must state that, although manual labour will have the effect of coating the hand with a rougher and thicker development of skin, yet it does not depress or decrease what are known as the mounts, and which, again, in their turn, show constitutional characteristics, which are doubtless caused by the hereditary laws which govern and control the intermingling of races. As regards the use by cheiromants of the old-time names, such as the Mount of Venus, Mars, etc., I must here state that I do not use these names in any sense in relation to what is known as Astrological Palmistry. I do not for one moment deny that there may be a connection—and a very great one—between the two; but I do not think it necessary to consider it in conjunction with this study of the hand, which study I hold to be in every way complete in itself. Consequently, I use such names as Venus, Mars, Saturn, etc., simply as a quicker way of giving the student an idea of the qualities I wish to describe. These qualities have been associated so long with such names in our minds as Mars, the martial nature, and so on, that their mere mention recalls them, and the employment of these terms will, therefore, simplify matters much more than if I were to call the mounts by numbers, as first, second, third, and so forth.

THE MOUNT OF VENUS

The Mount of Venus is the development found at the base of the thumb (Fig. 12). When not abnormally large it is a favourable sign on the hand of man or woman. This mount covers one of the largest and most important blood-vessels in the hand, the great palmar arch. Hence, if the Mount of Venus be well developed, it indicates strong and robust health. A small Mount of Venus betrays poor health, and consequently, less passion.

The Mount of Venus, abnormally large, indicates a violent passion for the opposite sex.

This mount denotes affection, sympathy toward others, benevolence, a desire to please, love and worship of beauty, love of colour, and melody in music, and the attraction of the one sex to the other.

THE MOUNT OF JUPITER

This mount is the raised formation at the base of the first finger (Fig. 12). When developed it shows ambition, pride, enthusiasm in anything attempted, and desire for power.

THE MOUNT OF SATURN

This is found at the base of the second finger (Fig. 12), and denotes love of solitude, quietness, prudence, earnestness in work, proneness to the study of sombre things, and appreciation of music of a sacred or classical order.

THE MOUNT OF THE SUN

This mount is found at the base of the third finger, and is also called the Mount of Apollo (Fig. 12). When well developed it indicates an enthusiastic appreciation of all things beautiful, whether or not one follows a purely artistic calling. It denotes love of painting, poetry, literature, and all imaginative work, also grace of mind and thought.

THE MOUNT OF MERCURY

The mount of this name is found at the base of the fourth finger (Fig. 12). It denotes all the mercurial qualities of life— love of change, travel, excitement, wit, quickness of thought and expression. If the rest of the hand is favourable, the

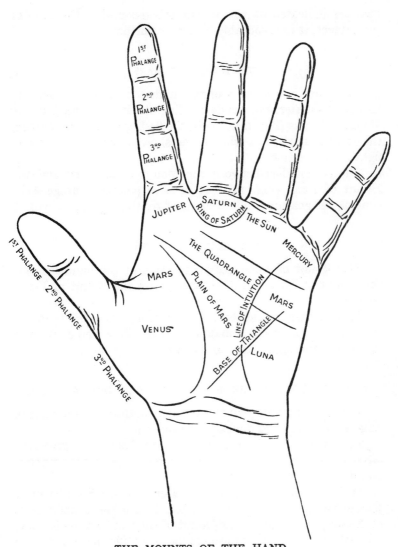

THE MOUNTS OF THE HAND

Fig. 12

qualities indicated by this mount will redound to the good of the subject, if unfavourable, to his misfortune.

THE MOUNT OF MARS

There are two mounts of this name; the first beneath the Mount of Jupiter, but inside the line of life, lying next to the Mount of Venus (Fig. 12). This, the first, gives active courage, the martial spirit, but when large, shows a very quarrelsome, fighting disposition.

The second lies between the Mount of Mercury and the Mount of Luna (Fig. 12). It denotes passive courage, self-control, resignation, and strength of resistance against wrong.

THE MOUNT OF LUNA

The Mount of Luna lies on the side of the hand beneath the Mount of Mars and directly opposite the Mount of Venus (Fig. 12).

It indicates refinement, imagination, love of beautiful scenery, a taste for the romantic, great ideality, and a fondness for poetry and imaginative literature.

THE LEANING OF THE MOUNTS TOWARD ONE ANOTHER

When the mounts lean toward one another, the qualities of each are blended and developed in unison.

For example, if Saturn lean toward Jupiter, it gives the latter some of its love of solemn things—its prudence, sadness, and its religious tendency.

If Saturn incline toward the Mount of the Sun, Saturn's solemn thoughts and ideas will blend with the artistic taste of the subject, and if the the Mount of the Sun lean to Mercury, art will influence the business or scientific nature of the individual.

"CHEIRO"
(*Pronounced Ki-ro*)

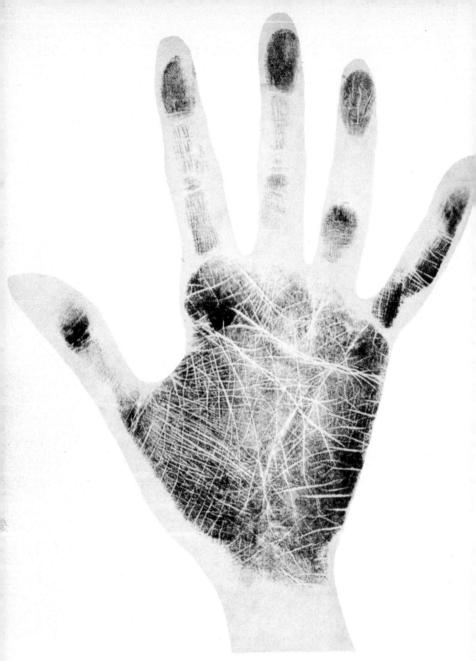

THE HAND OF H.H. THE INFANTA EULALIA

Plate II

For details see page 203

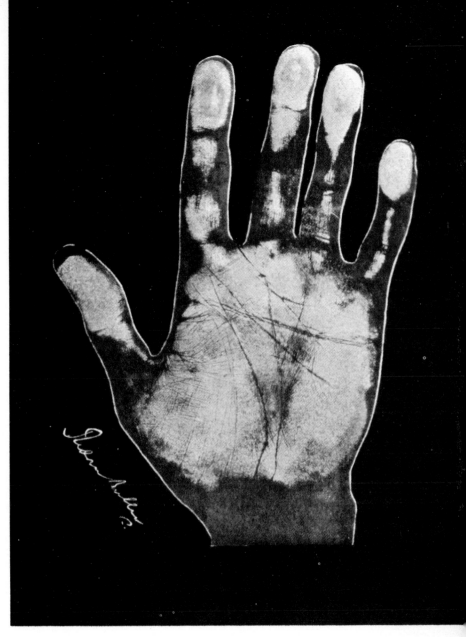

THE RIGHT HAND OF GEN. SIR REDVERS BULLER, V.C., G.C.B.

Plate III

For details see page 204

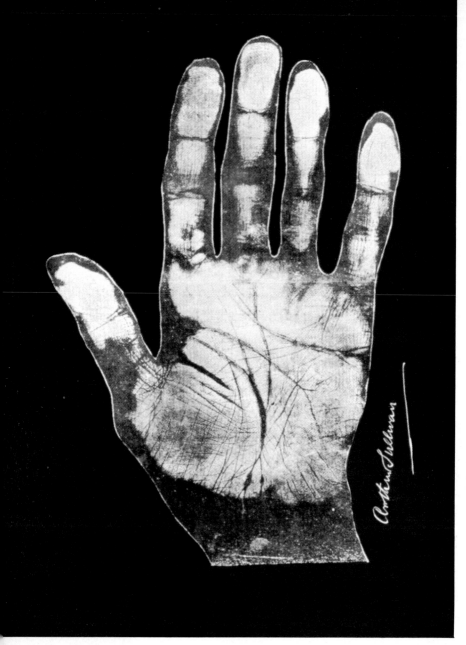

THE RIGHT HAND OF SIR ARTHUR SULLIVAN, Br.

Plate IV

For details see page 205

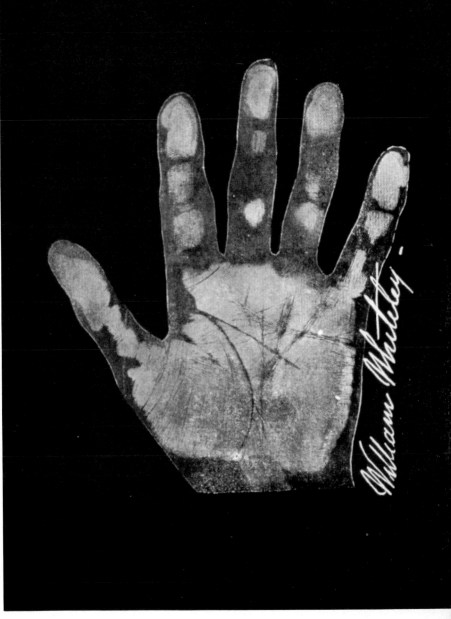

THE RIGHT HAND OF MR. WILLIAM WHITELEY

Plate V

For details see page 206

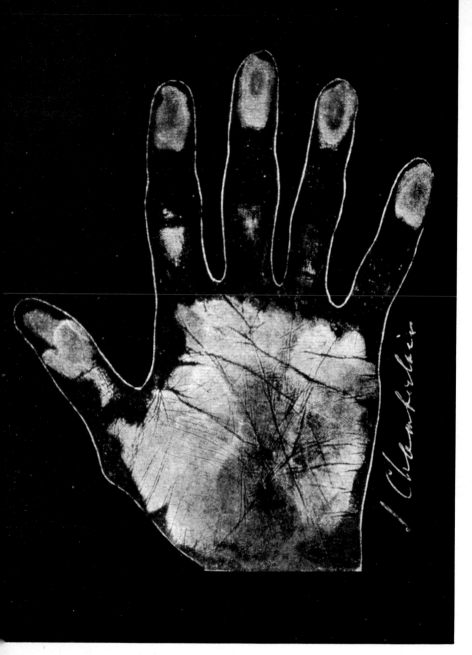

THE HAND OF THE RIGHT HON. JOSEPH CHAMBERLAIN, P.C.

Plate VI

For details see page 206

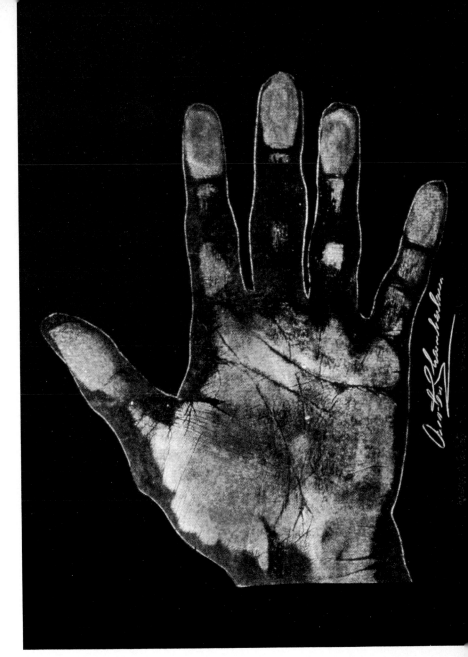

THE HAND OF RT. HON. SIR AUSTEN CHAMBERLAIN, K.G.

(Illustrative of hereditary tendencies, see hand of his father overleaf.)

Plate VII

For details see page 206

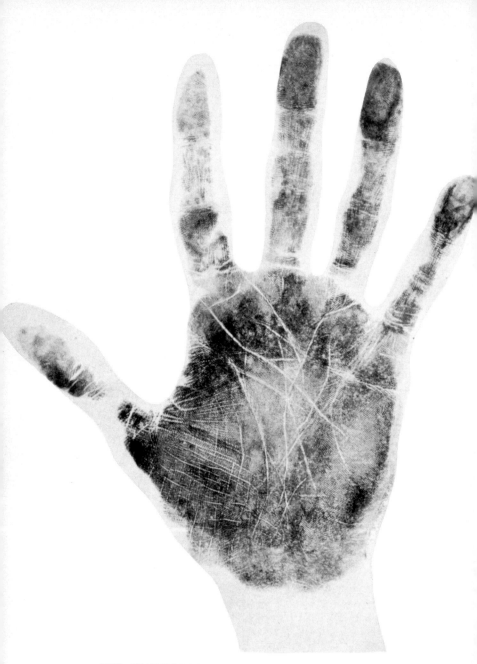

THE "DOUBLE LINE OF HEAD" "CHEIRO'S" HAND

Plate VIII

For details see page 207

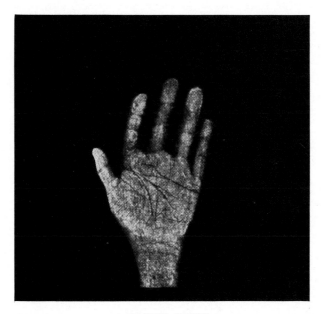

A BABY'S HAND

Plate IX

For details see page 208

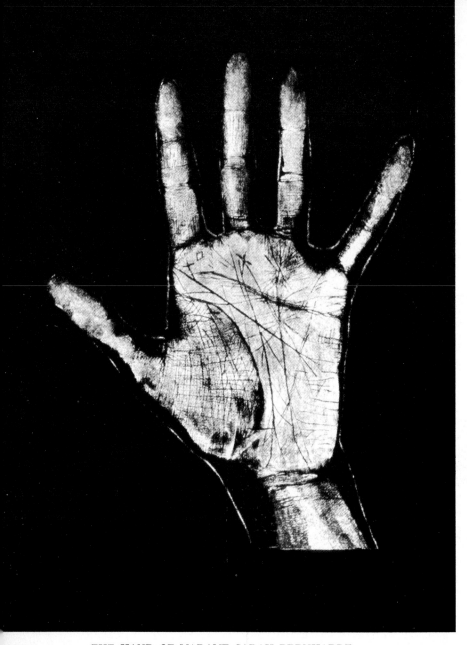

THE HAND OF MADAME SARAH BERNHARDT

Plate X

For details see page 208

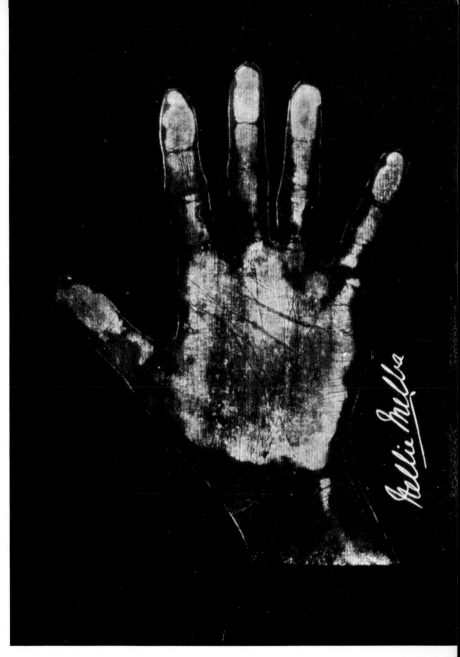

THE RIGHT HAND OF DAME NELLIE MELBA, G.B.E.

Plate XI

For details see page 209

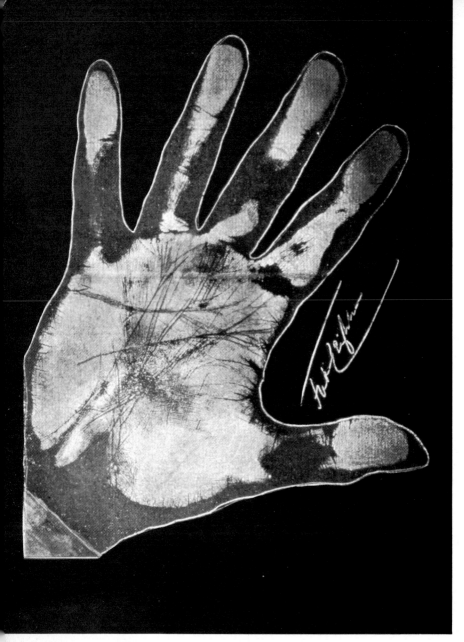

THE HAND OF LORD LEIGHTON, P.R.A.

Plate XII

For details see page 210

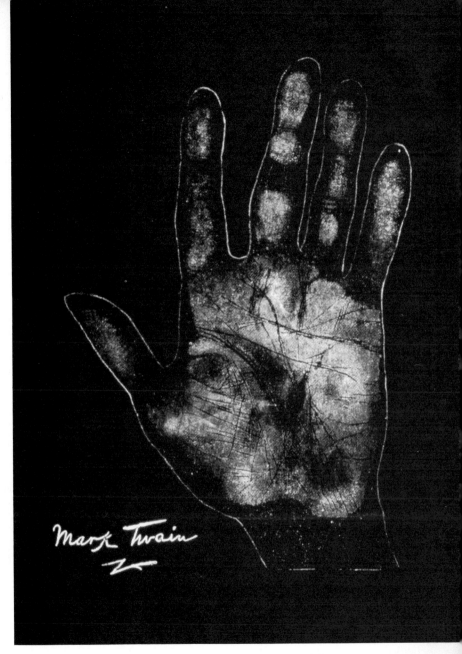

THE HAND OF MARK TWAIN

Plate XIII

For details see page 210

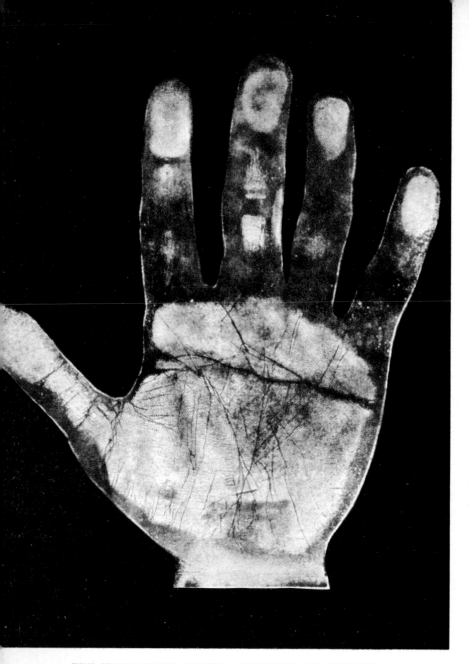

THE HAND OF DR. MEYER, CONVICTED OF MURDER

Plate XIV

For details see page 212

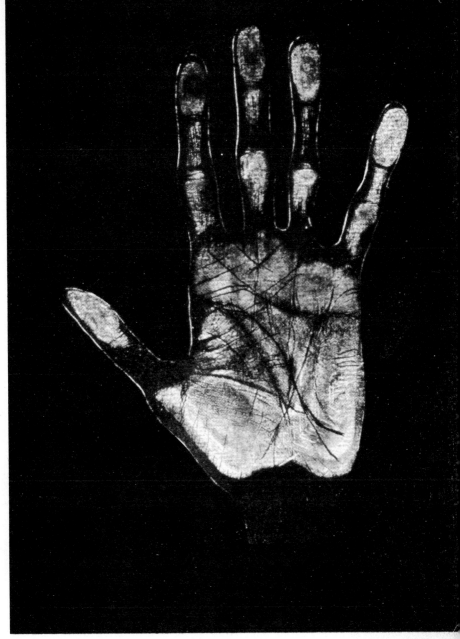

THE HAND OF A SUICIDE

Plate XV

For details see page 214

CHAPTER XVI

THE HANDS OF NATIONS

THAT different types of faces and bodies are characteristic of different nations is a well-known fact. There is a familiar statement which I would quote here: "The law which rounds a dewdrop shapes a world." Therefore, if certain laws produce different types in different races they also produce different shapes of hands and bodies as illustrative of the different characteristics. The intermingling and intermixing by marriage, etc., must naturally modify the pureness of the different types; but that it does not destroy the entire individuality cannot for a moment be doubted.

THE ELEMENTARY HAND

Starting with the elementary hand, it is rarely if ever found in its purity among civilized nations. We find this type among the primitive races in extremely cold latitudes, as, for instance, among the Esquimaux and the inhabitants of Iceland, Lapland, and the northern portion of Russia and Siberia.

Such people are phlegmatic and emotionless; even the nerve centres of the body are not in a high state of development, therefore they do not feel pain as keenly as the other types. They are more animal in their instincts and brutal in their desires; they are devoid of aspirations, and have only sufficient mentality to make them distinct from the brute creation. In a slightly more developed form the elementary hand is found in more southern and civilized nations.

THE SQUARE HAND AND THE NATIONS REPRESENTED BY IT

The square hand, generally speaking, is found among the Swedes, Danes, Germans, Dutch, English, and Scotch. The chief characteristics which it denotes are love of method, logic,

97

reason, respect for authority and law, and conformity to conventionality and custom.   It shows an undemonstrative and more or less unemotional nature; it will follow life's beaten track with dogged stubbornness and tenacity of purpose, will build solid houses, railways, and churches; will kneel at the shrine of the useful and will pay homage to the practical side of life.

THE PHILOSOPHIC

This is essentially the hand of the Oriental nations.   In European countries, it is to this type or to the possessors of its modifications that we are indebted for the modernized principles of Buddhism, Theosophy, and all doctrines and ideas that tend in that direction.   It is essentially the hand of the mystic or of the religious devotee.   Individuals with these hands will endure any privation or self-denial in defence of the religion they follow.   The world may call such people cranks; but the world crucified its Christ, and mocked and persecuted its greatest teachers.   Its opinion, therefore, should only affect the scales of dross, not the balance of thought.

THE CONIC

This type, properly speaking, is peculiar to the south of Europe, but by the intermingling of races it has been carried far and wide over the world.   It is largely found among Greek, Italian, Spanish, French, and Irish races.   The distinctive characteristics which it denotes are a purely emotional nature, impulse in thought and action, artistic feeling, impressionability and excitability.   It has been designated "The Hand of Impulse."   Such hands are not the hands of money-makers, like the square or the spatulate.   They show a lack of practical business sense, but nature compensates their owners with the poetic, the visionary, and the romantic.

THE SPATULATE

With all the varieties of national types that have found their way at some time or another to America; with all the admixture of races found in that enormous continent, the spatulate hand is the type which has to a great extent swallowed up

all the others. This hand, and, consequently, the characteristics that it represents, has to my mind played the importaut
rôle in the history of that great country. As I may claim to
be a cosmopolitan in every sense of the word, I can therefore
take an unbiassed standpoint in reading the character of nations
as I would that of the individual. The spatulate hand, as I
stated before, is the hand of energy, originality, and restlessness.
It is the hand of the explorer and the discoverer, which terms
can also be applied to discoveries in science, art, or mechanics.
Spatulate hands are never conventional; they have little respect
for law, less for authority. They are inventors, more from
the quickness of their ideas than from the solidity of earnest
work as exemplified by the square; they may utilize other men's
ideas, but they will try to improve upon.them; they love risk
and speculation; they are versatile, and their chief fault is their
changeability—they shift from one thing to another with the
mood of the moment; they are fanatics in their fads, enigmas in
their earnestness; but, even with such faults, it is to a people
many-sided and many-talented like this that the world must
look for her new ideas, for the inventions and discoveries in
science, religion, or materialism which must in years to come
work out the evolution of humanity.

THE PSYCHIC

This peculiar type is not confined to any particular country
or kindred; it is evolved sometimes among the most practical,
sometimes among the most enthusiastic. Yet is it neither
practical nor enthusiastic in itself; it may be an evolution of
all the types, reaching into that plane in which there may be
seven senses instead of five. Certain it is that its owners are
not of the earth, earthy, nor yet of heaven—for they are human;
they make up no distinct community, but are found in all and
of all. It may be that, as their beautiful hands are not formed
for the rough usage of this world, so their thoughts are not
suited to the material things of life. Their place may be in
giving to mankind that which is but the reflection of mankind.
Thus in the shadow may we find the substance and, in the
speculation that this type gives rise to, may we find that
wisdom which sees the fitness and the use of all things.

PART II: CHEIROMANCY

CHAPTER I

A FEW REMARKS IN REFERENCE TO THE READING OF THE HAND

BEFORE I proceed to explain the more intricate details of cheiromancy, I wish to address a few words to the student, as well as to the casual reader who may take sufficient interest in this study to glance through this book.

In the first place, in my earnest desire to make this work a thoroughly reliable guide in all matters connected with palmistry, I have been compelled to bring the details of the study prominently before the reader and to enlarge on certain points that may be considered dry and uninteresting. This the student may resent during the commencement of his enthusiasm, but later he will, I think, see its advantages, as I have endeavoured to make even the details as graphic as possible. I have not confined myself to the set theories of any particular school; I have gathered whatever information this book contains from, I may say, the four corners of the earth, and in presenting this information to those who desire to learn, I do so with the knowledge that I have proved whatever statements I make to be correct. The one point I would, however, earnestly desire to impress upon the student is the necessity for conscientious study and patience. As there are no two natures alike, so there are no two hands alike. To be able to read the hand is to be able to read the book of nature—there is no study more arduous, there is none more fascinating or that will repay the time and labour spent upon it with more interest.

To do this study justice, I cannot, and will not pretend, as do the generality of writers on this subject, that it is an easy matter, by following this, that, or the other map of the hand, or by taking some set rules as a guide, to be able to "read the hand" without any exercise of the student's mentality.   On the contrary, I shall show that every line, without exception, is modified by the particular type to which it belongs as, for instance, a sloping line of head on a square hand has a completely different meaning from the same sloping line on a conic, or philosophic type and so on.   I have written this book with the object of making it not only interesting to the reader, but useful to the student.   I have endeavoured to make every point as clear and concise as possible, but the student must bear in mind the enormous difficulties that lie in the way of making a clear explanation of every point in connection with such an intricate study.

The next point to be borne in mind is the difference of opinion which will be met with, and which is often used as an argument against palmistry.   Now we must remember that it is only through the concentration of different minds, and the concensus of different opinions, that we can ever hope to reach the truth on any subject.   No better illustration of this can be found than in the divergency of opinion that has existed and always will exist in religion, as well as in scientific study. What body of students have, or can have, more divergency of opinion, for instance, than medical men?   I must, therefore, say, in the words which a celebrated physician once used to his pupils, that we should, in the pursuit of any particular branch of study, take the teachings which we have the most reason to believe are correct, and that by building upon such a foundation we will attain greater heights of knowledge than the individual who follows every new teacher who for a moment, like the will-o'-the-wisp, flits across the shifting sands of human fancy.   Particularly in palmistry, I would say, take some work which you have good reason to believe is at least near the truth, and by following that out with the light of your own mentality and reason you will be more likely to succeed than those who, shifting their ground according to every fancy, find themselves at last without faith, without hope, and, worse still, without knowledge.

The chief point of difference between my teachings and those of other writers lies in the fact that I class the various lines under different heads, treating of each particular point.

This will be found not only more easy and less puzzling for

the student, but also more in accordance with reason. For instance, I hold that the line of life relates to all that affects life, to the influences which govern it, to its class as regards strength; to the natural length of life, and to the important changes of country and climate. I regard the line of head as related to all that affects mentality, and so on with every other line, as will be seen later. This plan I have found to be the most accurate, as well as the simplest, and more in accordance with those teachers whose ideas we have every reason to respect.

As regards dates, I depart from the usual formula, and instead advance a theory which has been considered "at least interesting and reasonable," in the dividing of the life into sevens, in accordance with the teachings of nature. I will illustrate this when I come to that portion of this work dealing with time and dates.

CHAPTER II

THE LINES OF THE HAND

THERE are seven important lines on the hand, and seven lesser lines (Fig. 13). The important lines are as follows:

The Line of Life, which embraces the Mount of Venus.
The Line of Head, which crosses the centre of the hand.
The Line of Heart, which runs parallel to that of the head, at the base of the fingers.
The Girdle of Venus, found above the line of heart and generally encircling the Mounts of Saturn and the Sun.
The Line of Health, which runs from the Mount of Mercury down the hand.
The Line of Sun, which rises generally on the Plain of Mars and ascends the hand to the Mount of the Sun.
The Line of Fate, which occupies the centre of the hand, from the wrist to the Mount of Saturn.

The seven lesser lines on the hand are as follows:

The Line of Mars, which rises on the Mount of Mars and lies within the Line of Life (Fig. 13).
The *Via Lasciva*, which lies parallel to the line of health (Fig. 13).
The Line of Intuition, which extends like a semi-circle from Mercury to Luna (Fig. 12).
The Line of Marriage, the horizontal line on the Mount of Mercury (Fig. 13), and
The three bracelets found on the wrist (Fig. 13).

The main lines are known by other names, as follows:

The Line of Life is also called the Vital.
The Line of Head, the Natural or Cerebral.
The Line of Heart, the Mensal.

The Line of Fate, the Line of Destiny, or the Saturnian.
The Line of Sun, the Line of Brilliancy, or Apollo.
The Line of Health, the Hepatica, or the Liver Line.

The hand is divided into two parts or hemispheres by the line of head.

The upper hemisphere, containing the fingers and Mounts of Jupiter, Saturn, the Sun, Mercury, and Mars, represents mind, and the lower, containing the base of the hand, represents the material.   It will thus be seen that with this clear point as a guide the student will gain an insight at once into the character of the subject under examination.   This division has hitherto been ignored, but it is almost infallible in its accuracy; as, for example, when the predisposition is toward crime the line of head rises into the abnormal position shown by Plate XIV, which, taken from life, is one instance in the thousands that can be had of the accuracy of this statement.

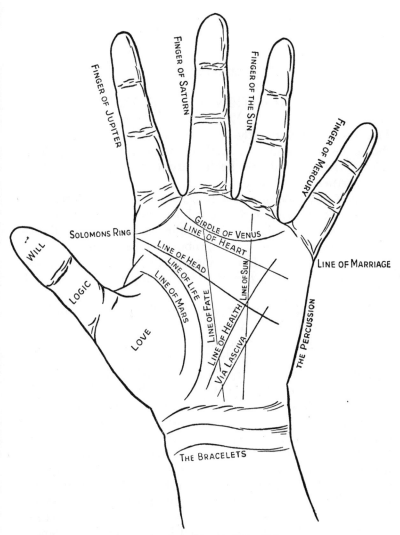

FINGER OF JUPITER

FINGER OF SATURN

FINGER OF THE SUN

FINGER OF MERCURY

SOLOMONS RING

GIRDLE OF VENUS

LINE OF HEART

LINE OF HEAD

LINE OF MARRIAGE

WILL

LOGIC

LINE OF LIFE

LINE OF MARS

LINE OF FATE

LINE OF HEALTH

LINE OF SUN

LOVE

VIA LASCIVA

THE PERCUSSION

THE BRACELETS

THE MAP OF THE HAND

Fig. 13

CHAPTER III

IN RELATION TO THE LINES

THE rules in relation to the lines are, in the first place, that they should be clear and well marked, neither broad nor pale in colour; that they should be free from all breaks, islands, or irregularities of any kind.

Lines very pale in colour indicate, in the first place, want of robust health, and, in the second, lack of energy and decision.

Lines red in colour indicate the sanguine, hopeful disposition; they show an active, robust temperament.

Yellow lines, as well as being indicative of biliousness and liver trouble, are indicators of a nature self-contained, reserved, and proud.

Lines very dark in colour, almost black, tell of a melancholy, grave temperament, and also indicate a haughty, distant nature, one usually very revengeful and unforgiving.

Lines may appear, diminish, or fade, which must always be borne in mind when reading the hand. The province of the palmist, therefore, is to warn the subject of approaching danger by pointing out the evil tendencies of his nature. It is purely a matter of the subject's will whether or not he will overcome these tendencies, and it is by seeing how the nature has modified evils in the past that the palmist can predict whether or not evils will be overcome in the future. In reading the hand, no *single* evil mark must be accepted as decisive. If the evil is important, almost every principal line will show its effect, and both hands must be consulted before the decision can be final. A single sign in itself only shows the tendency; when, however, the sign is repeated by other lines, the danger is then a certainty. In answer to the question, Can people avert or avoid danger or disaster predicted in the hand? I answer that decidedly I believe that they can; but I say just as decidedly that they rarely if ever do. I know hundreds of cases in my own experience where people were given accurate

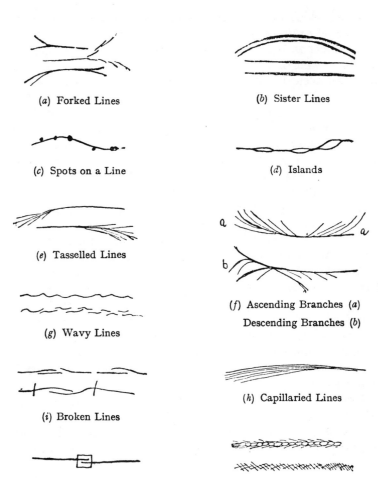

(a) Forked Lines

(b) Sister Lines

(c) Spots on a Line

(d) Islands

(e) Tasselled Lines

(f) Ascending Branches (a)
Descending Branches (b)

(g) Wavy Lines

(h) Capillaried Lines

(i) Broken Lines

(k) The Square on Line

(j) Chained Lines

LINE FORMATIONS

Fig. 14

warnings which they did not realize till too late. The most remarkable example of this which I can recall, occurred early in my career in the days of horse-drawn vehicles. It was the case of a woman well known in London society. I warned her of an accident caused by animals which would make her infirm for the rest of her life, and which would happen at the very point of age that she had then reached. She promised that she would be careful, and departed. A week later, one dull foggy night, she ordered her horses; again she got a warning, this time through her husband, who begged her not to go out, as the horses were restive and the night bad. The horses were brought round, and with them the last warning: her coachman had been taken seriously ill, and a substitute had to take his place. Even this did not deter her, and she started. The coachman could have gone any one of four different ways to reach his destination, but, strange to say, he took the most unlikely, and drove through Bond Street. It was in doing this that the most remarkable point in this example was reached. The man lost control of the horses; they took fright, and dashed on to the pavement; the carriage was smashed against a lamp-post, and, by an extraordinary coincidence, its occupant was carried, unconscious, into my own hall. I am sorry to say that the prediction proved only too true: she never recovered from her injuries.

I make no comment on this strange story; I simply relate the facts as they occurred.

The above is only one example in many that could be cited to show that we rarely if ever will go by warnings, no matter in what way they may be given.

When an important line, such as the line of head or of life, is found with what is called a sister line (Fig. 16, *a–a*), namely, a fine line running by its side, it is a sign that the main line is thus strengthened; consequently any break in the main line will be, as it were, bridged over by this mark, and the danger lessened or prevented. This is more often found in connection with the line of life than with any other.

If there is a fork at the end of any line, except that of life (Fig. 16), it gives greater power to that line; as, for instance, on the line of head it increases the mentality, but makes more or less of a double nature.

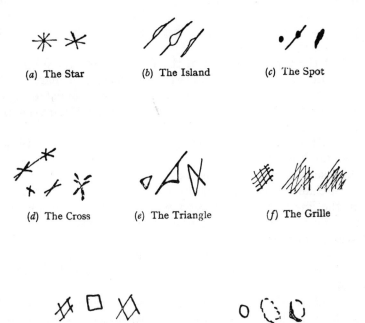

(a) The Star   (b) The Island   (c) The Spot

(d) The Cross   (e) The Triangle   (f) The Grille

(g) The Square   (h) The Circle

(i) The Trident and Spearhead

SIGNS FOUND IN THE HAND

Fig. 15

When, however, the line ends in a tassel (Fig. 16, *b–b*), it is a sign of weakness and destruction to any line of which it forms part, particularly at the end of the line of life, where it denotes weakness and the dissipation of all the nerve qualities.

Branches rising from any line (Fig. 14, *a–a*) accentuate its power and strength, but all branches descending denote the reverse.

At the commencement of the line of heart, these lines are most important when considering the success of marriage for the subject: the ascending lines at this point indicate vigour and warmth of the affections (Fig. 17, *a–a*); the descending, the opposite.

On the line of head ascending branches denote cleverness and ambitious talent (Fig. 16, *c–c*), and on the line of fate they show success in all undertakings made at that particular point.

A chained formation in any line is a weak sign (Fig. 14): if on the line of heart it denotes weakness and changeability of affection; if on the line of head, want of fixity of ideas, and weakness of intellect.

Breaks in any line denote its failure (Fig. 17, *c–c*).

A wavy formation weakens the power of the line (Fig. 17, *b–b*).

Capillary lines are those little hair-lines running by the side of the main line, sometimes joining it, sometimes falling from it; they denote weakness, like the chained formation (Fig. 14, *h*).

When the entire hand is covered with a network or multitude of little lines running aimlessly in all directions, it betrays mental worry, a highly nervous temperament, and a troubled nature.

As the little grains make mountains, so do these little points make this study great. I therefore recommend their close consideration.

CHAPTER IV

THE RIGHT AND LEFT HANDS

THE difference between the right and left hands is another important point to be considered. The most casual observer, looking at even a limited number of hands, is generally struck by the marked difference which as a rule exists in the shape and position of the lines in the right and left hands of the same person.

This is an important point to be observed by the student. In practice, my rule is to examine both hands, but to depend more upon the information given by the right than that given by the left.   There is a well-known old saying on this point: "The left is the hand we are born with; the right is the hand we make."   This is the correct principle to follow, the left hand indicating the natural character, and the right showing the training, experience, and the surroundings brought to bear on the life of the subject.   The old idea of reading the left hand simply because it is nearest to the heart belongs to the many superstitions which degraded the science in the Middle Ages. The heart at that time was regarded as the supreme organ— hence this medieval superstition.   If, however, we examine this study from a logical and scientific standpoint, we find that the greater use of the right hand for long generations has placed it, as regards both nerves and muscles, in a more perfect state of development than the left.   It is usually exercised in carrying out the thoughts of the brain, being, as it were, the more active servant of the mind.   If, therefore, as has been demonstrated, the human body passes through a process of slow and steady development, and every change it undergoes affects and marks its effect upon the entire sytem, it follows that it is more logical and reasonable to examine the right hand for those changes which even at that moment are taking place, and upon which the development of the future depends.

My advice, therefore, is: place both hands side by side;

examine them, and see what the nature has been, see what it is; find the reason by your examination for this or that change; and, in forecasting what will be, depend upon the development of the lines in the right hand.

It is very interesting to note that left-handed people have the lines more clearly marked on the left hand, and vice versa. Some people change so completely that hardly two lines are alike on both hands; again, some change so slightly that the difference in the lines is barely perceptible. The general rule to follow is, that when a marked difference is shown by both hands the subject has had a more interesting, eventful life than the person with both alike. The more interesting details as to a subject's past life, and even the very changes in his method of work and ideas, can be brought to light by a careful examination conducted in this way.

CHAPTER V

THE LINE OF LIFE

What we know as life is but existence,
A waiting-place, a haven by the sea,
A little space amid immeasured distance,
A glimpse, a vista, of that life to be.
CHEIRO.

As I remarked earlier, as there came to be recognized a natural position on the face for the nose, eyes, etc., so also on the hand there came to be recognized a natural position for the line of life, the line of head, and every other mark that the hand possesses. Thus, if the lines take abnormal courses it is only reasonable that abnormal characteristics are to be expected; and if so as regards temperament, why not in relation to health? People who consider this subject lightly object to the power given to the palmist in his ability to predict disease or death; but a little thought will show that nothing, after all, is more reasonable than one's ability to do this by careful study. It is admitted that in the body of every person there lurks a germ or tendency that will some day prove fatal. Who, therefore, can have the presumption to deny that this germ by its presence affects the nerve-fluid, which in its turn affects the nerves, and they the hand? Again, without touching on the presence in the body of the all-knowing, omnipotent soul or spirit life, if we acknowledge—as we do—the unexplained mysteries of the passive and active brain, we must also acknowledge that the slightest germ of disease or weak point in the system must be known to the brain in all its stages of advance and attack, and will, therefore, be registered by the brain on the hand through the nerve-connection between the two, as has already been demonstrated. Thus, by the development or non-development of this line or that mark is the palmist able to say that a certain disease at a certain time will cause illness with such and such a result. Bearing these arguments in mind, we will now proceed to an examination of what has become known as the line of life.

The line of life (Fig. 13), is the line which, rising under the Mount of Jupiter, goes down the hand and embraces the Mount of Venus. On it is marked time, also illness and death, and events foreshadowed by the other important lines are verified.

The line of life should be long, narrow, and deep, without irregularities, breaks, or crosses of any kind. Such a formation promises long life, good health, and vitality.

When the line is linked (Fig. 14, *j*) or made up of little pieces like a chain, it is a sure sign of bad health, and particularly so on a soft hand. When the line recovers its evenness and continuity, health also is regained.

When broken in the left hand and joined in the right, it threatens some dangerous illness; but if broken in both hands it generally signifies death. This is more decidedly confirmed when one branch turns back on the Mount of Venus (Fig. 17, *c–c*).

When the line starts from the base of the Mount of Jupiter, instead of the side of the hand, it denotes that from the earliest the life has been one of ambition.

When the line is chained at the commencement under Jupiter, bad health in early life is foreshadowed.

When the line is closely connected with that of the head, life is guided by reason and intelligence, but the subject is extremely sensitive about everything which affects self, and more or less cautious in enterprises for self (Fig. 16, *d–d*).

When there is a medium space between the line of life and that of head, the subject is more free to carry out his plans and ideas; it also denotes energy and a very go-ahead spirit (Fig. 17, *d–d*).

When, however, the space is very wide, it is a sign of too much self-confidence and dash; it indicates that the subject is foolhardy, impulsive, hasty, and not guided by reason.

When the lines of life, head, and heart are all joined together at the commencement (Fig. 18, *a–a*), it is a very unfortunate sign, denoting that the subject, through a defect in temperament, rushes blindly into danger and catastrophe. This mark, as far as temperament is concerned, indicates the subject's want of perception, both in personal dangers and in those arising from dealings with other people.

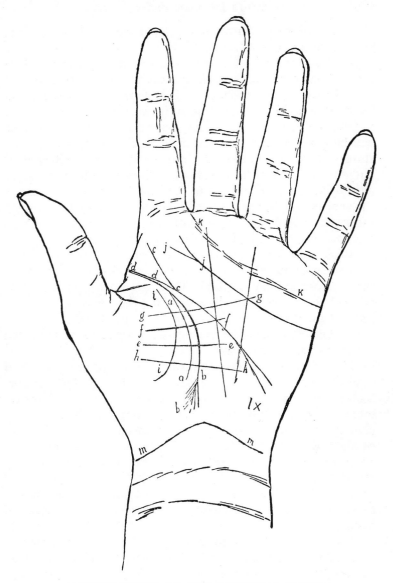

MODIFICATIONS OF THE PRINCIPAL LINES

Fig. 16

When the line of life divides at about the centre of the hand, and one branch shoots across to the base of the Mount of Luna (Fig. 18, *e–e*), it indicates on a firm, well-made hand a restless life, a great desire for travel, and the ultimate satisfaction of that desire. When such a mark is found on a flabby, soft hand, with a sloping line of head, it again denotes the restless nature, craving for excitement, but in this case the craving will be gratified in vice or intemperance of some kind. This statement, as will be seen, can be logically and easily reasoned out; the line crossing to the Mount of Luna denotes the restless nature craving for change, but, the hand being soft and flabby, the subject will be too lazy and indolent to satisfy this craving by travel, and the sloping line of head in this case showing a weak nature, the reason for this statement is apparent.

When little hair-lines are found dropping from or clinging to the line of life, they tell of weakness and loss of vitality at the date when they appear. They are very often found at the end of the line itself, thus denoting the breaking up of the life and the dissipation of vital power (Fig. 16, *b–b*).

All lines that rise from the line of life are marks of increased power, gains, and successes.

If such a line ascend toward or run into the Mount of Jupiter (*Fig.* 18, *c–c*), it will denote a rise in position or step higher at the date it leaves the line of life. Such a mark relates more to successful ambition in the sense of power than anything else. If the line, on the contrary, rise to Saturn and follow by the side of the line of fate, it denotes the increase of wealth and worldly things, but resulting from the subject's own energy and determination (Fig. 18, *d–d*).

If the line leave the line of life and ascend to the Mount of the Sun, it denotes distinction according to the class of hand.

If it leave the line of life and cross to Mercury, it promises great success in business or science, again in accordance with the class of hand—whether square, spatulate, or conic. For instance, such a line on the square would indicate success in business or science; on the spatulate, in invention or discovery; and on the conic it would foretell success in money matters, reached by the impulsive action of such a nature, as in sudden speculation or enterprise.

When the line of life divides toward the end and a wide space is shown between the lines, it is an indication that the subject will most probably end his life in a country different from that of his birth, or at least that there will be some great change from the place of birth to the place of death (Fig. 19, *a–a*).

An island on the line of life means an illness or loss of health while the island lasts (Fig. 19, *b*), but a clearly formed island at the commencement of the line of life denotes some mystery connected with the subject's birth.

The line running through a square (Fig. 19, *c*), indicates preservation from death, from bad health when it surrounds an island, from sudden death when the life-line running through is broken, and from accident when a little line cutting the life-line rises from the Plain of Mars (Fig. 19, *d*).

A square, whenever found on the line of life, is a mark of preservation.

Of the great attendant line (Fig. 13) found parallel to and within the line of life, otherwise called the line of Mars, I shall speak later. This attendant line, the line of Mars, which rises on the Mount of Mars, must not be confounded with those springing from the line of life itself, nor with those that rise upon the Mount of Venus. The simplest rule to bear in mind is, that all even, well-formed lines following the line of life indicate favourable influences over the life (Fig. 17, *f–f*), but that all those rising in the opposite direction and cutting the life-line show worries and obstacles caused by the opposition and interference of others (Fig. 17, *g–g*). Where these lines end and how they terminate is, therefore, an important point in this study.

When they cut the line of life only (Fig. 17, *g–g*), they denote the interference of relatives—generally in the home life.

When they cross the life-line and attack the line of fate (Fig. 16, *e–e*), they denote people who will oppose us in business or worldly interests, and where they cut the fate-line the point of junction gives the date.

When they reach the line of head (Fig. 16, *f–f*), they indicate persons who will influence our thoughts and interfere with our ideas.

When they reach and cut the line of heart (Fig. 16, *g–g*),

they denote interference in our closest affections, and here the date of such interference is given where the line cuts the life-line, and not where it touches the line of heart.

When they cut and break the line of sun (Fig. 16, *h–h*), they denote that others will interfere and spoil our position in life, and that the mischief will be caused by scandal or disgrace at the point of junction.

When the line crosses the hand and touches the line of marriage (Fig. 17, *h–h*), it signifies divorce, and will occur to the person on whose hand it appears.

When this crossing-line has in itself a mark like an island or any approach to it, it denotes that the person who will cause the trouble has had either scandal or some such trouble in connection with his or her own life (Fig. 17, *i*).

When, on the contrary, the ray-lines run parallel as it were to attend the life-line, they denote the most important influences of our lives (Fig. 17, *f–f*).

I draw special attention to this system, as it prevails among the Hindus, and dating back to time immemorial. The following points have been obtained by close study of the precepts and their practical application by the Hindus themselves, and not a few of them have been translated almost verbatim from the quaint leaves of that ancient work before mentioned. When minuteness of detail is required, the remarkable accuracy of this system makes it especially valuable.

I will give the leading points only, as the subject is well-nigh inexhaustible.

In the first place, if the ray-line rise on the Mount of Mars (Fig. 18, *e–e*), and lower down touch or attack the life-line in any way, it denotes on a woman's hand some unfavourable attachment in her early life which will cause her much trouble and annoyance.

If the same line, however, send only offshoots or rays to the line of life (Fig. 18, *f–f*), it denotes a similar influence, but one that will continue to persecute her at different intervals. Again, such a line on a woman's hand is illustrative of the nature of the man who influences her, as denoting a fiery, passionate, animal temperament.

If, however, the ray-line should rise by the side of the line of life and travel by the side of it (Fig. 17, *f–f*), it shows, on the

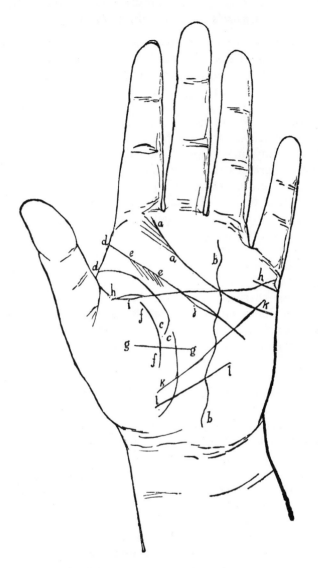

MODIFICATIONS OF THE PRINCIPAL LINES

Fig. 17

woman's hand, that the man who enters into her life has the gentler nature, and that she will strongly influence him.

If the ray-line, rising at any point, in travelling with the life-line, retreats farther in on the Mount of Venus, thus away from the life, it indicates that the person with whom the woman is connected will more and more lose sympathy with her, and will eventually drift out of her life altogether (Fig. 16, *i–i*).

When the ray-line, however, runs into an island or becomes one itself, it foretells that the influence over her life will run into disgrace, and that something scandalous will result.

When the attendant line fades out by the side of the life-line, but renews itself later, it tells that the person influencing the life will cease his influence at that particular point, but that it will be renewed again.

When the line of influence fades altogether, total separation —generally death—will be the result of such companionship.

When one of these attendant lines joins a cross-line and runs over the hand with it, it foretells that through the instrumentality of another the affection of the person influencing the life will change to hate, and that this will cause injury at whatever point it touch the life, the fate, the head, or the line of heart (Fig. 19, *e–e*).

The farther the ray-lines lie from the line of life, the farther removed from our lives will those influences be. But, as before remarked, one could easily fill a volume on these lines and cross-lines, which with the Hindus are the foundation for all systems connected with palmistry.

By this system alone, then, it is reasonable to assume that the student can predict marriages by considering the relation which these lines bear to the life-line. We will again refer to this point when we consider the question of marriage.

Another interesting phase of this subject is the consideration of the number of these lines of influence (it being remembered that only those near the line of life are important). Numerous lines indicate a nature dependent upon affection. Such people are what is called passionate in their disposition; they may have many *liaisons*, but in their eyes love redeems all. On the other hand, the full, smooth Mount of Venus indicates that the individual is less affected by those with whom he is associated.

When the line of life sweeps far out into the hand, thus allowing the Mount of Venus a greater scope, it is in itself a sign of good physical strength and long life.

When, on the contrary, it lies very close to the Mount of Venus, health is not so robust or the body physically so well built. The shorter the line the shorter the life.

That the line of life does not *always* show the exact age at which death takes place I am quite convinced. This line merely denotes the natural term of the subject's life apart from accidental influences. Catastrophes indicated by other lines of the hand may cut short a life that would otherwise be long. For instance, a break in the head-line at certain points, as explained in Chapter VII, will foretell death just as surely as would the broken life-line. Again, and most important of all, the slope and position of the line of health in relation to the life-line is a point which hitherto has not received the attention it deserves. When we consider the line of health, the relation that these lines bear to one another will be treated in detail. I may, however, here remark that, when it is of equal strength with that of life, where these lines meet will be the point of death, even though it be years in advance of when the life-line ends. Such a death will be caused by whatever disease is indicated by the health-line, and the province and one of the many uses of this study is to find out and warn the subject of that germ of disease which is even then the enemy of the system.

In addition to the information I have given here concerning islands, squares, etc., I refer the student back to Chapter III, which treats of them more fully. As regards time and the calculation of events, a special chapter will be devoted to these subjects.

CHAPTER VI

THE LINE OF MARS

THE line of Mars (Fig. 13) is otherwise known as the inner vital or inner life-line. It rises on the Mount of Mars, and sweeps down by the side of the line of life, but is distinct in every way from those faint lines known as the attendant lines, of which I spoke a little earlier.

The general characteristic of the line of Mars is that it denotes excess of health on all square or broad hands; to a man of this type it gives a martial nature, rather a fighting disposition, and robust strength. It also denotes that while it runs close to the life-line the individual will be engaged in many quarrels, and will be subject to a great deal of annoyance which will bring all his martial or fighting qualities into play. It is always an excellent sign on the hand of a soldier.

When a branch shoots from this line out to the Mount of Luna (Fig. 20, b–b), it tells that there is a terrible tendency toward intemperance of every kind, through the very robustness of the nature, and the craving for excitement that it gives.

The other type of the line of Mars is found on the long, narrow hand, and here it is generally by the side of a delicate, fragile line of life. Its characteristics in such a hand are that it supports the life line, carrying it past any dangerous breaks, and giving vitality to the nature.

A broken line of life with such a line beside it will, at the point of the break, indicate closeness to death, but helped by this mark the subject will recover, through the great vitality given by the line of Mars.

CHAPTER VII

THE LINE OF HEAD

"To know is power"—let us then be wise,
  And use our brains with every good intent,
That at the end we come with tired eyes
  And give to Nature more than what she lent.

CHEIRO.

THE line of head (Fig. 13) relates principally to the mentality of the subject—to the intellectual strength or weakness, to the temperament in its relation to talent, and to the direction and quality of the talent itself.

It is of extreme importance in connection with this line that the peculiarities of the various types be borne in mind; as, for instance, a sloping line of head on a psychic or conic hand is not of half the importance of a sloping line on a square hand. We will, however, take general characteristics first, and proceed to consider variations afterward.

The line of head can rise from three different points—from the centre of the Mount of Jupiter, from the commencement of the line of life, or from the Mount of Mars, within the life-line.

Rising from Jupiter (Fig. 20, c–c) and yet touching the line of life, it is, if a long line of head, the most powerful of all. Such a subject will have talent, energy, and daring determination of purpose, with boundless ambition combined with reason. Such a man will control others, yet not seem to control them; he will have caution even in his most daring designs; he takes pride in his management of people or things, and is strong in rule, but just in the administration of power.

There is a variation of this which is almost equally strong. This again rises on Jupiter, but is slightly separated from the line of life. Such a type will have the characteristics of the first, but with less control and diplomacy. He will be hasty in decision, impetuous in action. As a leader in a crisis such a man would find his greatest opportunity. When, however, the space is very wide, the subject will be foolhardy, egotistical, and will rush blindly into danger.

The line of head from the commencement of the line of life, and connected with it (Fig. 16, *d–d*), indicates a sensitive and more nervous temperament; it denotes excess of caution; even clever people with this mark rein themselves down too tightly.

The line of head rising from the Mount of Mars, within the life-line (Fig. 19, *f–f*), is not such a favourable sign, it being the extreme on the inside of the life-line, as the wide-spaced head-line is the extreme on the outside. This indicates a fretful, worrying temperament, inconstant in thought, inconstant in action; the shifting sands of the sea are more steadfast than are the ideas of such an individual, and the connection with Mars gives his nature this one disagreeable trait—he is always in conflict with his neighbours; he is also highly sensitive, nervous, and more or less irritable.

The generalities indicated by the line of head are as follows:

When straight, clear, and even, it denotes practical common sense and a love of material things more than those of the imagination.

When straight in the first half, then slightly sloping, it shows a balance between the purely imaginative and the purely practical; such a subject will have a level-headed, common-sense way of going to work, even when dealing with imaginative things.

When the entire line has a slight slope, there is a leaning toward imaginative work, the quality of such imagination denoting, in accordance with the type of hand, either music, painting, literature, or mechanical invention. When very sloping, romance, idealism, imaginative work, and Bohemianism. When sloping, and terminating with a fine fork on the Mount of Luna, it promises literary talent of the imaginative order.

When extremely long and straight, and going directly to the side of the hand (the percussion), it usually denotes that the subject has more than ordinary intellectual power, but is inclined to be selfish in the use of that power.

When this line lies straight across the hand and slightly curves upward on Mars (Fig. 19, *g–g*), the subject will win unusual success in a business life; such a man will have a keen sense of the value of money—it will accumulate rapidly in his hands. Such a sign, however, denotes the taskmaster of life— the Pharaoh who expects his work-people to make bricks without straw.

When the line is short, barely reaching the middle of the hand, it tells of a nature that is thoroughly material. Such a man will utterly lack all the imaginative faculties, although in things practical he will be quite at home.

When abnormally short, it foreshadows some early death from some mental affection.

When broken in two under the Mount of Saturn, it tells of an early sudden death by fatality.

When linked, or made up of little pieces like a chain, it denotes want of fixity of ideas, and indecision.

When full of little islands and hair-lines, it tells of great pain to the head and danger of brain disease.

When the line of head is so high on the hand that the space is extremely narrow between it and the line of heart, the head will completely rule the heart, if that line be the strongest, and vice versa.

If the line should turn at the end, or if, in its course down the hand, it sends an offshoot or branch to any particular mount, by so doing it partakes of the qualities of that mount:

Toward the Mount of Luna, imagination, mysticism, and a leaning toward occult things.

Toward Mercury, commerce or science.

Toward the Sun, the desire for notoriety.

Toward Saturn, music, religion, and depth of thought.

With a branch to Jupiter, pride and ambition for power.

If a branch from the line of head rises up and joins the line of heart, it foreshadows some great fascination, or affection, at which moment the subject will be blind to reason and danger.

A double line of head is very rarely found, but when found it is a sure sign of brain power and mentality. Such people have a perfectly double nature—one side sensitive and gentle, the other confident, cold, and cruel. They have enormous versatility, great command of language, a peculiar power for playing and toying with human nature, and generally great will and determination.

When the line of head is broken in two on both hands, it foretells some fatal accident or violence to the head.

An island is a sign of weakness (Fig. 17, *j*). When clearly defined, if the line does not extend farther, the person will never recover.

If the line of head sends an offshoot to or runs into a star on the Mount of Jupiter, it is a sign of wonderful success in all things attempted.

When a number of little hair-lines branch upward from the line of head to that of heart, the affections will be a matter of fascination, not of love.

When the line of head runs into or through a square, it indicates preservation from accident or violence by the subject's own courage and presence of mind.

When there is a space found between the line of head and that of life, it is beneficial when not too wide; when medium, it denotes splendid energy and self-confidence, promptness of action and readiness of thought (Fig. 21, *f–f*). This is a useful sign for barristers, actors, preachers, etc., but people with such a mark would do well to sleep on their decisions—they are inclined to be too hasty, self-confident, and impatient. When this space is extremely wide, it denotes foolhardiness, assurance, excessive effrontery, and self-confidence.

When the line of head, on the contrary, is very tightly connected with that of life, and low down in the hand, there is utter want of self-confidence. Such individuals suffer greatly from extreme sensitiveness, and the slightest thing will wound and grieve them.

CHAPTER VIII

THE LINE OF HEAD IN RELATION TO THE SEVEN TYPES

THE general rules to be observed in connection with this most remarkable point are as follows:

The line of head is usually in accordance with the type of hand on which it is found—namely, practical on a practical type, imaginative on an artistic, and so on. It therefore follows that signs contrary to the nature are more important than characteristics indicated in accordance with it.

These peculiarities, it is therefore more reasonable to assume, relate to the development of the brain outside and beyond its natural characteristics. Such a divergence might be accounted for by the theory that the various tendencies of the brain reach their working point through a process of slow growth and development, similar to the evolutions of life itself. It therefore follows that at the age of twenty there may be the commencement of a development which may alter the entire life at thirty; but as that change has already commenced in the brain, so must it affect the nerves and thus the hand. Thus a tendency toward a change of thought or action is indicated years before it takes place.

Starting with the elementary hand, or the nearest approach to it found in our country, the natural head-line on such a type would be short, straight, and heavy; consequently the development of it to any unusual extent will show unusual characteristics in such a subject. For instance, such a line of head dropping downward toward Luna will show an imaginative but superstitious tendency, completely at variance with the brutal and animal nature it influences. This accounts for the fear of the unknown, the superstitious dread that is so often found among the lower class of humanity, particularly among savage tribes.

THE LINE OF HEAD IN RELATION TO THE SQUARE HAND

The square hand, as I have stated (Part I, Chapter III), is the useful or practical hand; it deals with logic, method, reason, science, and all things appertaining to such matters.

The line of head on such a type is straight and long, in keeping with the characteristics of the hand itself. It therefore follows that the slightest appearance of this line sloping, being the direct opposite to the nature, shows even a greater development of the imaginative faculties than a far greater slope of the same line on a conic or psychic, but the difference in the class of work would be the difference of temperament. The square hand with the sloping head-line would start with a practical foundation for imaginative work, whereas the other would be purely inspirational and imaginative. This difference is extremely noticeable in the hands of writers, painters, musicians, etc.

THE LINE OF HEAD IN RELATION TO THE SPATULATE HAND

The spatulate hand (Part I, Chapter IV) is the hand of action, invention, independence, and originality. The natural position for the line of head on this type is long, clear, and slightly sloping. When, therefore, on such a hand this sloping is accentuated, the result is that all these characteristics are doubled or strengthened; but when lying straight, the opposite of the type, the subject's practical ideas will keep the others so much in check that the plans of the imagination will not get scope for fulfilment, and, as far as the temperament is concerned, the nature will be restless, irritable, and dissatisfied.

THE LINE OF HEAD IN RELATION TO THE PHILOSOPHIC HAND

The philosophic hand (Part I, Chapter V), is thoughtful, earnest in the pursuit of wisdom, but imaginative and rather eccentric in the application of ideas to everyday life. The natural position for the line of head on this type is long, closely connected with the line of life, set low down on the hand, and sloping. The unnatural type, or the man with the straight line of head on the philosophic hand, the line set high on the hand and straight, is critical, analytical, and cynical; he will pursue wisdom, and particularly the study of his fellow men, only to analyse their faults and failings, to expose their fads, fancies, and foibles; he will stand on the border-land of the mystic, to sneer at the unreal, to laugh in the face of the real; he will fear nothing, neither things spiritual nor things material; he can be imaginative or practical at will; a genius that discredits genius, a philosopher that disarms philosophy—such is the hand of a Carlyle.

THE LINE OF HEAD IN RELATION TO THE CONIC HAND

The conic hand (Part I, Chapter VI) belongs to the artistic, impulsive nature, the children of ideas, the lovers of sentiment.

In this type the natural position for the line of head is that which gradually slopes downward to the Mount of Luna, generally to the middle of it. This is the most characteristic, and gives the freedom of Bohemianism to these worshippers of the beautiful; here it is that we find the greatest leaning toward sentiment, romance, and ideality, in opposition to the practical qualities of the square type. These are, indeed, the luxurious children of the Sun; they have a keen appreciation for the things of art, but are often without the power to give expression to their artistic ideas. However, when the line of head is straight, in combination with such a nature, a very remarkable result follows. The subject with such a hand will make every use of his artistic ideas and talents, but in a practical direction; he will intuitively feel what the public demands; he will not care for art so much as for the money it brings; he will conquer the natural love of ease and luxury by strength of common-sense and determination; where the man with the sloping head-line would paint one picture he will paint ten—and, furthermore, he will sell them. Why? Because through his practical business sense he will know what the public wants, and as is the demand, so will be the supply.

THE LINE OF HEAD IN RELATION TO THE PSYCHIC HAND

The natural position for the line of head on this hand is extremely sloping, giving all the visionary, dreamy qualities in accordance with this type. It is one of the rarest things to find a straight line of head on such a hand, but when found it is generally on the right hand, the left being still very sloping. Such a formation denotes that by the pressure of circumstances the entire nature has undergone a change and has become more practical. This type, even with the straight line of head, can never be very material or business-like, but in matters of art the subject will have a very good chance, as he would have more opportunity to exercise his talents, yet even in art it would require the greatest tact and strongest encouragement to induce him to turn his talents to practical use.

By such illustrations the student will understand how to make every other modification in accordance with the type of hand. The modifications of the head-line are more important than any other marks that the hand possesses.

CHAPTER IX

INSANITY AS SHOWN BY THE LINE OF HEAD

THERE is really no tendency which the hand denotes more plainly than insanity, whether hereditary or brought on by circumstances. The multitude of forms which could be gathered under this heading cannot be entered into in this work, but I will endeavour to show the most general.

It must be borne in mind that any point that is beyond the normal is abnormal. When, therefore, the line of head sinks to an abnormal point on the Mount of Luna, the imagination of the subject is abnormal and unnatural. This will be more important in the elementary, square, spatulate, and philosophic, than in relation to the conic or psychic types. When the line of head, even on a child's hand, reaches this unnatural point, it may grow up to manhood or womanhood with perfect clearness and sanity of ideas, but as surely as a mental shock or strain comes, so surely will that brain be thrown off its balance, and insanity will be the result.

The same development of the line of head, with an unusually high Mount of Saturn, will denote a morbidly imaginative nature from the very start (Plate XV). Such a subject is gloomy, morose, and melancholy, and this tendency, even without cause, generally increases until the subject completely loses his or her mental balance.

Temporary insanity is shown by a narrow island in the centre of a sloping line of head, but this mark generally indicates some brain-illness or temporary insanity consequent upon brain-fever.

The hand of the congenital idiot is remarkable for its very small, badly-developed thumb, and for a line of head sloping and made up of broad lines filled with a series of islands, like a chain.

I have further illustrated these remarks in Part III, Chapter V, on various phases of insanity as shown by the hand.

MURDEROUS PROPENSITIES AS SHOWN BY THE LINE OF HEAD

The mere act of murder, such as one man killing another in the heat of passion, or in self-defence, is not shown by the hand except as a past event, and then only when it has deeply affected a very sensitive nature; but if propensities for crime exist, the age at which they will reach their active or working point in the nature is decidedly shown, as I will proceed to demonstrate.

I have explained in the foregoing remarks that, when the line of head is abnormal in one direction, abnormal characteristics are the result, such as insanity, morbidness, and extreme melancholy, which under certain conditions lead to self-murder. These, however, are abnormal characteristics denoted by the falling line. We will now consider the abnormalities indicated by the rising line of head.

It will be remembered that I have previously stated that the line of head divides the hand into two hemispheres—that of mind and that of matter; and that if it be high on the hand, then the world of matter has greater scope, and the subject is more brutal and animal in his desires. This has been amply proved by the hands of those who have lived a life of crime, particularly if they have been murderous in their propensities (Plate XIV).

In such cases the line of head leaves its proper place on the hand and rises and takes possession of the line of heart, and sometimes even passes beyond it. Whether such people murder one or twenty is not the question. The point is that they have abnormal tendencies for crime; they stop at nothing in the accomplishment of their purpose, and under the slightest provocation or temptation they must and will gratify these strange and terrible propensities. The extraordinary thing in connection with this point is that the same line also predicts years in advance when these propensities will cause the destruction of the subject. If the head and heart meet under Saturn, it will occur before he is twenty-five; between Saturn and the Sun, before thirty-five; under the Mount of the Sun, before forty-five; and so on. This is one of the most interesting points in the study of the hand, and goes far to prove that, once the line of head goes over or under what should be its normal position, it betrays these various inherent tendencies in the character and the nature of the subject. In this way it will be seen that this study could be used to the greatest advantage in the training of children and young persons, as the line of head from the earliest indicates the mental bent of the subject whether for good or evil. There can be no doubt but that nature points in some way, even years in advance, to the harvest of those seeds that we are continually sowing; let us then look facts in the face whether they speak against ourselves or our children. Humanity has little pity for the reaper when binding the sheaves of regret: he cries, I did not know the seeds that I had sown.

(NOTE.—I do not use or pay attention to such signs as the red cross on Mars or the black spot on Saturn as indications of murder. I consider that they belong to the more superstitious side of this work, and are relics of that black age which once claimed palmistry as its own.)

CHAPTER X

THE LINE OF HEART

... Keep still, my heart,
Nor ask for peace, when care may suit thee best,
Nor ask for love, nor joy, nor even rest,
But be content to love, whate'er betide,
And maybe love will bring thee to Love's side.

CHEIRO.

THE line of heart is naturally an important line in the study of the hand. Love, or the attraction of the sexes from natural causes, plays one of the most prominent parts in the drama of life, and as in the nature so in the hand. The line of heart, otherwise called the mensal (Fig. 13), is that line which runs across the upper portion of the hand at the base of the Mounts of Jupiter, Saturn, the Sun, and Mercury.

The line of heart should be deep, clear, and well coloured. It may rise from three important positions, as follows: the middle of the Mount of Jupiter, between the first and second fingers, and from the centre of the Mount of Saturn.

When it rises from the centre of Jupiter (Fig. 20, *d–d*), it gives the highest type of love—the pride and the worship of the heart's ideal. A man with such a formation is firm, strong, and reliable in his affections; he is as well ambitious that the woman of his choice shall be great, noble, and famous—such a man would never marry beneath his station, and will have far less love-affairs than the man with the line from Saturn.

Next we will consider the line rising from the Mount of Jupiter, even from the finger itself (Fig. 20, *e–e*). This denotes the excess of all the foregoing qualities; it gives the blind enthusiast, the man so carried away by his pride that he can see no faults, no failings in that being whom he so devotedly worships. Alas! such people are the sufferers in the world of affection: when their idols fall, as idols will sometimes, the shock to their pride is so great that they rarely if ever recover from its effects; but the shock, it must be remarked, is more to their own pride than to the mere fact that the idol they worshipped had feet of clay. Poor worshipper! when wilt thou see that, though women be pure, they be not perfect; they are but human, and being human they are more fitting than if they were divine. Why, then, place them so high that they are the more likely to fall? Their place is by thy side, the companion of thy humanity, the sister part of all thy faults.

The line rising between the first and second fingers gives a calm but deeper nature in matters of love (Fig. 20, *f-f*). Such individuals seem to rest between the ideality given by Jupiter and the passionate ardour given by Saturn. They are quieter and more subdued in their passions.

With the line of heart rising from Saturn, the subject will have more passion in his attachments, and will be more or less selfish in satisfying his affections; in home life he is never so expressive or demonstrative as are those with the line from Jupiter. The excess of this is the same kind of line rising very high on the mount, often from the very finger of Saturn. Such a subject is far more passionate and sensual than any of the others. It is generally admitted that very sensual people are very selfish—in this case they are extremely so.

When the line of heart is itself in excess, namely, lying right across the hand from side to side, an excess of affection is the result, and a terrible tendency toward jealousy; this is still more accentuated by a very long line of heart rising to the outside of the hand and reaching the base of the first finger.

When the line of heart is much fretted by a crowd of little lines rising into it, it tells of inconstancy, flirtations, a series of *amourettes*, but no lasting affection (Fig. 20).

A line of heart from Saturn, chained and broad, gives an utter contempt for the subject's opposite sex.

When the line of heart is bright red, it denotes great violence of passion.

When pale and broad, the subject is *blasé* and indifferent.

When low down on the hand and thus close to the line of head, the heart will always interfere with the affairs of the head.

When, however, it lies high on the hand, and the space is narrowed by the line of head being too close, the reverse is the case, and the head will so completely rule the affections that it gives a hard, cold nature, envious and uncharitable.

Breaks in the line tell of disappointment in affection—under Saturn, brought about by fatality; under the Sun, through pride; and under Mercury, through folly and caprice.

When the line of heart commences with a small fork on the Mount of Jupiter (Fig. 16, *j–j*), it is an unfailing sign of a true, honest nature and enthusiasm in love.

A very remarkable point is to notice whether the line of heart commences high or low on the hand. The first is the best, because it shows the happiest nature.

The line lying so low that it droops down toward the line of head is a sure sign of unhappiness in affections during the early portion of the life.

When the line of heart forks, with one branch resting on Jupiter, the other between the first and second fingers, it is a sign of a happy, tranquil nature, good fortune, and happiness in affection; but when the fork is so wide that one branch rests on Jupiter, the other on Saturn, it then denotes a very uncertain disposition, and one that is not inclined to make the marital relations happy, through its erratic temperament in affection.

When the line is quite bare of branches and thin, it tells of coldness of heart and want of affection.

When bare and thin toward the percussion or side of the hand, it denotes sterility.

Fine lines rising up to the line of heart from the line of head denote those who influence our thoughts in affairs of the heart, and by being crossed or uncrossed denote if the affection has brought trouble or has been smooth and fortunate.

When the lines of heart, head and life are very much joined together, it is an evil sign; in all matters of affection such a subject would stick at nothing to obtain his or her desires.

A subject with no line of heart, or with very little, has not the power of feeling very deep affection. Such a person can, however, be very sensual, particularly if the hand is soft. On a hard hand such a mark will affect the subject less—he may not be sensual, but he will never feel very deep affection.

When, however, the line has been there, but has faded out, it is a sign that the subject has had such terrible disappointments in affection that he has become cold, heartless, and indifferent.

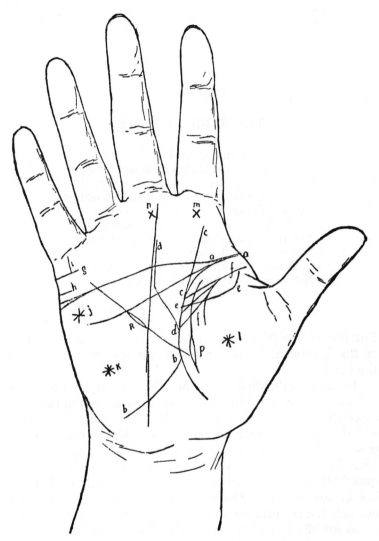

MODIFICATIONS OF THE PRINCIPAL LINES

Fig. 18

CHAPTER XI

THE LINE OF FATE

... And what is fate?
A perfect law that shapes all things for good;
And thus, that men may have a just reward
For doing what is right, not caring should
No earthly crown be theirs, but in accord
    With what is true, and high, and great.
And in the end—the part as to the whole—
So shall all be; in the success of all
So shall all share; for the All-conscious Soul
Notes e'en the sparrow's feeble fall.
    ... And such is fate.

CHEIRO.

THE line of fate (Fig. 13), otherwise called the line of destiny, or the Saturnian, is the centre upright line on the palm of the hand.

In the consideration of this line the type of hand plays an important part; for instance, the line of fate, even in the most successful hands, is less marked on the elementary, the square, and the spatulate, than on the philosophic, the conic, or the psychic. These upright lines are more in keeping with the latter hands, and are therefore less important on them; consequently if one sees, as one often will, an apparently very strong line of fate on a conic hand, one must remember that it has not half the importance of a similar line on a square type as far as worldly success is concerned. This point, I am sorry to say, has been completely overlooked by other writers, though it is one of the most significant in this study. It is useless simply to give a map of the hand without clearly explaining this point. The bewildered student sees this long line of fate marked as a sign of great fortune and success, and naturally concludes that a small line on the square hand means nothing, and that a long one on the conic or psychic means success, fame, and fortune, whereas it has not one quarter the importance of the small line shown on the square. I wish to emphasize this as so many students throw up palmistry in despair through not having this point explained at the start.

The strange and mysterious thing to note is that the possessors of the philosophic, conic, and psychic hands which bear these heavily marked lines are more or less believers in fate, whereas the possessors of the square and spatulate rarely, if ever, believe in fate at all.

Before the student goes farther I would recommend him, once and for all, to settle this doctrine of fate, either for or against.

The line of fate, properly speaking, relates to all worldly affairs, to our success or failure, to the people who influence our career, whether such influences be beneficial or otherwise, to the barriers and obstacles in our way, and to the ultimate result of our career.

The line of fate may rise from the line of life, the wrist, the Mount of Luna, the line of head, or even the line of heart.

If the fate-line rise from the line of life and from that point on is strong, success and riches will be won by personal merit; but if the line be marked low down near the wrist and tied down, as it were, by the side of the life-line, it tells that the early portion of the subject's life will be sacrificed to the wishes of parents or relatives (Fig. 20, *g–g*).

When the line of fate rises from the wrist and proceeds straight up the hand to its destination on the Mount of Saturn, it is a sign of extreme good fortune and success.

Rising from the Mount of Luna, fate and success will be more or less dependent on the fancy and caprice of other people. This is very often found in the case of public favourites.

If the line of fate be straight and a branch run in and join it from the Mount of Luna, it is somewhat similar in its meaning—it signifies that the strong influence of some other person, out of fancy, or caprice, will assist the subject in his or her career. On a woman's hand, if this ray-line from Luna travel on afterward by the side of the line of fate, it denotes a wealthy marriage or influence which accompanies and assists her (Fig. 20, *h–h*).

If the line of fate in its course to the Mount of Saturn send offshoots to any other mount, it denotes that the qualities of that particular mount will dominate the life.

If the line of fate itself should go to any mount or portion of the hand other than the Mount of Saturn, it foretells great success in that particular direction, according to the characteristics of the mount.

If the line of fate ascend to the centre of the Mount of Jupiter, unusual distinction and power will come into the subject's life. It also relates to character. Such people are born to climb up higher than their fellows through their enormous energy, ambition, and determination.

If the line of fate should at any point throw a branch in that direction, namely, toward Jupiter, it shows more than usual success at that particular stage of life.

If the line of fate terminate by crossing its own mount and reaching Jupiter, success will be so great in the end that it will go far toward satisfying even the ambition of such a subject.

When the line runs beyond the palm, cutting into the finger of Saturn, it is not a good sign, as everything will go too far. For instance, if such an individual be a leader, his subjects will some day go beyond his wishes and power, and will most probably turn and attack their commander.

When the line of fate is abruptly stopped by the line of heart, success will be ruined through the affections; when, however, it joins the line of heart and they together ascend Jupiter, the subject will have his or her highest ambition gratified through the affections (Fig. 19, *h–h*).

When stopped by the line of head, it foretells that success will be thwarted by some stupidity, or blunder of the head.

If the line of fate does not rise until late in the Plain of Mars, it denotes a very difficult, hard, and troubled life; but if it goes on well up the hand, all difficulties will be surmounted, and once over the first half of the life all the rest will be smooth. Such success comes from the subject's own energy, perseverance and determination.

If the line of fate rise from the line of head, and that line be well marked, then success will be won late in life, after a hard struggle and through the subject's talents.

When it rises from the line of heart extremely late in life, after a difficult struggle success will be won.

When the line rises with one branch from the base of Luna, the other from Venus, the subject's destiny will sway between imagination on the one hand and love and passion on the other (Fig. 21, *m–m*).

When broken and irregular, the career will be uncertain; the ups and downs of success and failure full of light and shadow.

When there is a break in the line, it is a sure sign of misfortune and loss; but if the second portion of the line begin before the other leaves off, it denotes a complete change in life, and if very decided it will mean a change more in accordance with the subject's own wishes in the way of position and success (Fig. 22, *a–a*).

A double or sister fate-line is an excellent sign. It denotes two distinct careers which the subject will follow. This is much more important if they go to different mounts.

A square on the line of fate protects the subject from loss through money, business, or financial matters. A square touching the line in the Plain of Mars (Fig. 21, *b*), foretells danger from accident in relation to home life if on the side of the fate-line next the line of life; from accident in travel if on the side of the fate-line next the Mount of Luna.

A cross is a sign of trouble and follows the same rules as the square, but an island in the line of fate is a mark of misfortune, loss, and adversity (Fig. 21, *d*). It is sometimes marked with the line of influence from Luna, and in such a case means loss and misfortune caused by the influence, be it marriage or otherwise, which affects the life at that date (Fig. 21, *c*).

People without any sign of a line of fate are often very successful, but they lead more a vegetable kind of existence. They eat, drink, and sleep, but I do not think we can really call them happy, for they cannot feel acutely, and to feel happiness we must also feel the reverse. Sunshine and shadow, smiles and tears comprise the sum total of our lives.

CHAPTER XII

THE LINE OF SUN

And there are some who have success in wealth,
And some in war, and some again in peace,
And some who, gaining their success in health,
   See other things decrease.
Man can't have all—the sun consumes itself
By burning in its lap more feeble stars,
And those who crave the Hindu idol's part
Oft crush their children 'neath their gilded cars.
                                        CHEIRO.

THE line of sun (Fig. 13), otherwise called the line of Apollo,
the line of brilliancy, or the line of success, must, like the line
of fate, be considered with the type of hand on which it lies;
for instance, it will be more heavily marked on the philosophic,
conic, and psychic, and not mean as much as a similar line
on the square or spatulate.   The same rule given in reference
to the line of fate therefore applies to this.

I prefer in my work to call this the line of sun, as this name
is more expressive and more clear in meaning.   It increases
the success given by a good line of fate, and gives fame and
distinction to the life when it is in accordance with the work
and career given by the other lines of the hand; otherwise it
merely relates to a temperament that is keenly alive to the
artistic, but unless the rest of the hand bears this out, the
subject will have the appreciation of art without the power of
expression.

The line of sun may rise from the line of life, the Mount of
Luna, the Plain of Mars, the line of head, or the line of heart.

Rising from the line of life, with the rest of the hand artistic,
it denotes that the life will be devoted to the worship of the
beautiful.   With the other lines good, it promises success in
artistic pursuits.

Rising from the line of fate, it increases the success promised

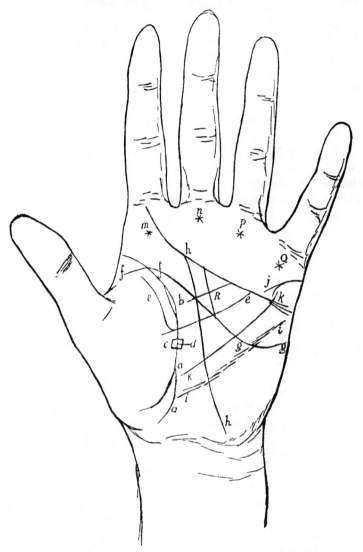

MODIFICATIONS OF THE PRINCIPAL LINES

Fig. 19

by the line of fate, and gives more distinction from whatever date it is marked—from that time on things will greatly improve.

It is far more accurate and less misleading to class this line as relating to brilliancy or success—as its name implies—than to call it the line of Apollo or of art.   It depends upon the talent shown by the line of head, and the class of hand itself, to determine in what way the success is shewn, whether in art or in riches.

From the Mount of Luna it promises success and distinction, largely dependent upon the fancies and the help of others.   In this case it is never a certain sign of success, being so influenced by the fortunes of those with whom we come in contact (Fig. 21, *e–e*).

With a sloping line of head, however, it is more inclined to denote success in poetry, literature, and things of the purely imaginative order.

Rising upon the Plain of Mars, it promises sunshine after tears, success after difficulty.

Rising from the line of head, there is no caprice of other people in connection with success, the talents of the subject alone being its factor, but not until the second half of life is reached.

Rising from the line of heart it merely denotes a great taste for art and artistic things, and looking at it from the purely practical standpoint it denotes more distinction and influence in the world at that late date in life.

If the third finger be nearly equal in length to the second, the finger of Saturn, a very long line of sun with such a formation makes the subject inclined to gamble with everything— the talents, the riches, and even the chances of life.

The chief peculiarity of this line is that it generally gives, when well marked, a great tendency toward sensitiveness, but when combined with an exceptionally straight line of head it denotes the love of attaining riches, social position, and power.

Many lines on the Mount of Sun show an extremely artistic nature, but multiplicity of ideas will interfere with all success. Such subjects never have sufficient patience to win either fame or renown (Fig. 21).

A star on this line is perhaps the very finest sign that can be found. Brilliant and lasting success is in such cases a certainty.

A square on the line of sun is a sign of preservation against the attacks of enemies in reference to one's name and position (Fig. 21, *g*).

An island on this line means loss of position and name for the length of time that the island lasts, and generally such will occur through scandal (Fig. 21, *h*).

On a hollow hand the line of sun loses all power.

The complete absence of the line of sun on an otherwise talented and artistic hand indicates that such people, though they may work hard, will find the recognition of the world difficult to gain. Such individuals, no matter how they may deserve honour and fame, will rarely achieve it. Perhaps on their graves will be laid the wreaths that should have crowned their heads.

CHAPTER XIII

THE LINE OF HEALTH, OR THE HEPATICA

> Some flowers are bruised that they may be more sweet,
> And some lie broken 'neath the rush of feet;
> And some are worn awhile, then tossed aside;
> Some grace the dead, while others deck the bride.
> And so in life I've seen the saddest face,
> The broken flower, give forth the sweetest grace.
>
> CHEIRO.

THERE has been considerable discussion among writers as to the point where this line rises. My theory, and one which I have proved by watching the growth of this line on the hands of children and young people, is that it rises at the base, or on the face of the Mount of Mercury, and as it grows down the hand and into the line of life, so does it foreshadow the growth of the illness or germ of disease which at the time of its coming in contact with the line of life will reach its climax. I wish to call special attention to this point; also to another, namely, that the line of life merely relates to the length of life from natural causes, but if the hepatica is as strongly marked as the line of life itself, their meeting at any point will be the point of death. Also, no matter how long the life-line may seem to be, any abnormal development of the line of health will cause the death of the subject.

The hepatica (Fig. 13) should lie straight down the hand—the straighter the better.

It is an excellent sign to be without this line. Such absence denotes an extremely robust, healthy constitution. Its presence on the hand in any form indicates some delicate point to be guarded against.

When crossing the hand and touching the line of life at any point, it tells that there is some delicacy at work, undermining the health and constitution (Fig. 17, k–k).

When rising from the line of heart at the Mount of Mercury and running into or through the line of life, it foretells some weakness and disease of the heart.   If very pale in colour, and broad, it will be weak action of the heart and bad circulation.

If red in colour, particularly when it leaves the line of heart, with small, flat nails, the trouble will be active heart-disease.

When very red in small spots, it denotes a tendency in the system toward fever.

When twisted and irregular, biliousness and liver complaints.

When formed in little straight pieces, bad digestion (Fig. 19, *i–i*).

In little islands, with long, filbert nails, danger to lungs and chest (Fig. 20, *i–i*).

The same mark, with the same kind of nail, but broad, throat trouble.   (See "Nails," Part I, Chapter XIII.)

When heavily marked, joining the line of heart and head, and not found elsewhere, it threatens brain-fever.

A straight line of hepatica lying down the hand may not give robust health, but it is a good mark because it gives a more wiry kind of health than one crossing the hand.

It will thus be seen that though the student can depend very largely upon the indications afforded him by the hepatica, yet he must look for other illnesses, and for confirmation of illnesses, to other portions of the hand, as, for instance, to the chained life-line for naturally delicate health, to the line of head for brain troubles, and to the nails, which must always be noted in conjunction with the study of the hepatica.

CHAPTER XIV

THE VIA LASCIVA AND THE LINE OF INTUITION

THE *Via Lasciva*, otherwise called the sister health-line (Fig. 13), is not often found, and is generally confounded with the hepatica. It should run off the palm into the wrist. In such a position it gives action and force to the passions, but if running across the hand into the Mount of Venus it shortens the natural length of life by its excesses (Fig. 17, *l–l*).

THE LINE OF INTUITION

The line of intuition (Fig. 12) is more often found on the philosophic, the conic, and the psychic, than on any other of the seven types. Its position on the hand is almost that of a semicircle from the face of the Mount of Mercury to that of the Mount of Luna. It sometimes runs through or with the hepatica, but can be found clear and distinct even when the hepatica is marked. It denotes a purely impressionable nature, a person keenly sensitive to all surroundings and influences, an intuitional feeling of presentiment for others, strange vivid dreams and warnings which science has never been able to account for by that much-used word, "coincidence." It is found more on psychic hands than on any others.

CHAPTER XV

THE GIRDLE OF VENUS, THE RING OF SATURN, AND THE THREE BRACELETS

THE Girdle of Venus (Fig. 13) is that broken or unbroken kind of semicircle rising between the first and second fingers and finishing between the third and fourth.

I must here state that I have never found this sign to indicate the sensuality so generally ascribed to it, except when found on a broad, thick hand. Its real domain is usually on such hands as the conic and psychic. A little study will prove that this mark is as a rule associated with highly sensitive intellectual natures, but natures changeable in moods, easily offended, and touchy over little things. It denotes a highly strung, nervous temperament, and when unbroken it certainly gives a most unhappy tendency toward hysteria and despondency.

People possessing this mark are capable of rising to the highest pitch of enthusiasm over anything that engages their fancy, but they are rarely twice in the same mood—one moment in the height of spirits, the next miserable and despondent.

When the girdle goes over the side of the hand and by so doing comes in contact with the line of marriage (Fig. 16, *k–k*), the happiness of the marriage will be marred through the peculiarities of the temperament. Such subjects are peculiarly exacting, and hard to live with. If on a man's hand, that man would want as many virtues in a wife as there are stars in the universe.

THE RING OF SATURN

The Ring of Saturn (Fig. 12) is a mark very seldom found, and is not a good sign to have on the hand. I have closely watched people possessing it, and I have never yet observed that they were in any way successful. It seems to cut off the Mount of Fate in such a peculiar way that such people never gain any point that they may work for or desire. Their temperament has a great deal—it may have everything—to do with this, as I always find these people full of big ideas and plans, but with such want of continuity of purpose that they always give up half-way. (See also Plate XV.)

THE THREE BRACELETS

The bracelets (Fig. 13) I do not consider of much importance in reading the lines, or in the study of the hand itself. There is, however, one strange and peculiar point with regard to them, and one that I have noticed contains a great deal of truth. I had been taught in my early life, always to observe principally the position of the first bracelet, the one nearest the hand, and that when I saw it high on the wrist, almost rising into the palm, particularly when it rose in the shape of an arch (Fig. 16, *m–m*), I was always to warn my consultant of weakness in relation to the internal organs of the body—as, for instance, in the bearing of children. Afterwards in my life, when I took up this study in a more practical way, I found there was a great deal of truth in what I at first thought a superstition. In later years, by watching case after case, by going through hospitals, and from what my many consultants have told me in reference to their ailments, I have become convinced that this point deserves being recorded, and consequently I now give it for what it may be worth.

Another significance attached to the bracelets is that, if well and clearly defined, they mean strong health and a robust constitution, and this again, it is interesting to notice, bears out in a manner the point I have called attention to.

CHAPTER XVI

THE LINE OF MARRIAGE

What matter if the words be said,
The licence paid—they are not wed;
Unless love link each heart to heart,
'Twere better keep those lives apart.
CHEIRO.

OF the many books that have been written on cheiromancy, I
am sorry to say that almost all have ignored or have barely
noticed this naturally interesting and important point.   I will
therefore endeavour to give as many details as possible in
connection with this side of the study.

What is known as the line or lines of marriage, as the case
may be, is that mark or marks on the Mount of Mercury as
shown by Fig. 13.   It must be first stated, and stated clearly,
that the hand does not recognize the mere fact of a ceremony,
be it civil or religious—it merely registers the influence of
different people over our lives, what kind of influence they have
had, the effect produced, and all that is in accordance with
such influence.   Now, marriage being so important an event in
one's life, it follows that, if events can be foretold by the hand,
marriage should certainly be marked, even years in advance,
and I have always found that such is the case in respect to all
important influences; and it is also natural that *affaires de
cœur, liaisons*, and so on, can thus be singled out and divided
from what is known as marriage, except when the *liaison* is
just as important and the influence on the life just as strong.
Why there should be a time set apart in one's life to marry, or
not to marry, as the case may be, can only be answered by
referring to the other mysteries that surround us.   If anyone
can explain why a permanent magnet brought into an ordinary
room has the power to magnetize every other bit of iron in the
room, what that power is, and what the connection is, then he
may be able to answer the question; but until all the secret

laws and forces of nature are known, we can take no other standpoint than to accept these strange anomalies without having the power to answer the cry of the curious, the perpetual parrot-like "Why?" of the doubting. The only theory I advance is that, as the press of the finger on the telegraph keyboard in New York at the same moment affects the keyboard in London, so by the medium of the ether, which is more subtle than electricity, are all persons unconsciously in touch with and in communion with one another.

In studying this point of the subject, I wish to impress upon the student that what are known as the lines of marriage must be balanced by marks on other portions of the hand, as I have shown by the influences by the side of the line of fate (Part II, Chapter XI), and by the lines of influence by the side of the line of life (Part II, Chapter V).

We will now proceed with the marks in connection with these lines of marriage on the Mount of Mercury.

The line or lines of marriage may rise on the side of the hand or be only marked across the front of the Mount of Mercury.

Only the long lines relate to marriages (Fig. 18, *g*); the short ones to deep affection or marriage contemplated (Fig. 18, *h*). On the line of life or fate, if it be marriage, we will find it corroborated and information given as to the change in life, position, and so on. From the position of the marriage-line on the Mount of Mercury a very fair idea of the age at the time of marriage may also be obtained.

When the important line is found lying close to the line of heart, the union will be early, about fourteen to twenty-one; near the centre of the mount, about twenty-one to twenty-eight; three-quarters up the mount, twenty-eight to thirty-five; and so on. But the line of fate or the line of life will be more accurate, by giving almost the exact date of the change or influence.

A wealthy union is shown by a strong, well-marked line from the side of the line of fate next Luna (Fig. 20, *h–h*), running up and joining the line of fate, when the marriage-line on Mercury is also well marked.

When, however, the line of influence rises first straight on the Mount of Luna and then runs up and into the fate-line, the marriage will be more the capricious fancy than real affection.

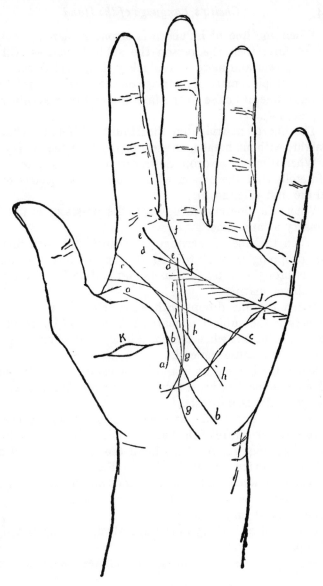

MODIFICATIONS OF THE PRINCIPAL LINES

Fig. 20

When the line of influence is stronger than the subject's line of fate, then the person the subject marries will have greater power and more individuality than the subject.

The happiest mark of marriage on the line of fate is when the influence-line lies close to the fate-line and runs evenly with it (Fig. 20, *l–l*).

The line of marriage on the Mount of Mercury should be straight, without breaks, crosses, or irregularities of any kind.

When it curves or drops downward toward the line of heart, it foretells that the person with whom the subject is married will die first (Fig. 20, *j*).

When the line curves upward, the possessor is not likely to marry at any time.

When the line of marriage is distinct, but with fine hair-lines dropping from it toward the line of heart, it foretells trouble brought on by the illness and bad health of the person the subject marries.

When the line droops with a small cross over the curve, the person the subject is married to will die by accident or sudden death; but when there is a long, gradual curve, gradual ill-health will cause the end.

When the line has an island in the centre or at any portion, it denotes some very great trouble in married life, and a separation while the island lasts.

When the line divides at the end into a drooping fork sloping toward the centre of the hand, it tells of divorce or a judicial separation (Fig. 19, *j*). This is all the more certain if a fine line cross from it to the Plain of Mars (Fig. 19, *k–k*).

When the line is full of little islands and drooping lines, the subject should be warned not to marry. Such a mark is a sign of the greatest unhappiness.

When full of little islands and forked, it is again a sign of unhappiness in marriage.

When the line breaks in two, it denotes a sudden break in the married life.

When the line of marriage sends an offshoot on to the Mount of Sun and into the line of sun, it tells that its possessor will marry someone of distinction, and generally a person in some way famous.

When, on the contrary, it goes down toward and cuts the

line of sun, the person on whose hand it appears will lose
position through marriage (Fig. 21, *i–i*).

When a deep line from the top of the mount grows downward and cuts the line of marriage, there will be a great
obstacle and opposition to such marriage (Fig. 18, *i*).

When there is a fine line running parallel with and almost
touching the marriage-line, it tells of some deep affection after
marriage on the side of the person on whose hand it appears.

It is not within my province in this work on palmistry to
go deeply into my opinions as to the laws relating to marriage,
or to marriages as entered into by men and women of the
present day. It is almost incredible what men and women
have told me during the pursuit of this study. They generally
say, "You have read so much, you may as well now know all,"
and so they unravel the greatest secrets of their hearts. The
palmist's lips are sealed, as are those of the father confessor,
but if he did speak he would tell that half the smiling faces
are but masks of gaiety to hide hearts of woe, that half the
so-called truths are falsehoods cloaked, that half the vows are
mockeries, and that the greatest mockery of all is, alas! too
often, that so-called ceremony of marriage. The Protestant
Church allows its children to be divorced if the marriage has
turned out unsuitable, and yet the last words dinned into the
ears of the bride and bridegroom are, "Those Whom God hath
joined together, let no man put asunder." The Catholic
Church, equally inconsistent, will not even allow the wretched
pair to divorce and marry again unless on certain special
occasions through the "mediation of the Pope," and on the
other hand the divorce courts pour back into the coffers of the
State that which is in reality the blood-money of its citizens.
How long, how long will this lip-service dethrone and crush the
service of the heart? How long will this slavery of custom
degrade and destroy the better nature, making men brutes
and women beasts of burden? How long must men and
women exist and live together because they have not the
money to buy their freedom, or because of their dread of that
torture-chamber of divorce? Men who were noble once, women
who were queens of truth and souls of honour—how often do
we see them, the husband hating the wife, the wife fearing the
husband, and outside of all and seeing all, like the spectators

in the arena, are the pale faces of the children, the reincarnated ghosts of buried faith, edging closer and closer to the scene, fearing too much, loving too little, wrapping around them, closer than their very garments, the cloak of parents' shame, going out into the world to deceive as mother did, to drink as father did—going out into the world to do likewise.

Let men and women, once and for all, read nature more and fiction less; let them study one another as they do the art of flattery or of costume. Let them marry, but if they make mistakes, give them a chance of redeeming those mistakes; give them children, but teach them to be responsible to those children; preach not goodness for the sake of gain, but goodness for the sake of good; honour for honour's sake, truth for truth's. And lastly, give them pride, not in self—for they are servants—but in that part of life in which they serve, that as they be sons of humanity and daughters of the world, so may they live as helpers of the world. And so may they be till the end draws nigh, till the task is done, till the universe is finished, till the destiny is spun.

CHAPTER XVII

CHILDREN

> . . . So oft to bear,
> Thro' early hours, thro' later years,
> The story of a mother's tears
> Or of a father's drunken care.
> Ah me! how hard
> To bear that load, that heavy cross,
> To stagger on, and, stumbling, find
> All life but death, all death but loss,
> With eyes alone to virtue blind!
>
> Cheiro.

To tell accurately the number of children one has had, or is likely to have, seems a very wonderful thing to do, but it is not one bit more wonderful than the details given by the main lines. To do this, however, requires more careful study than is usually given to the pursuit of cheiromancy.

Owing to the accuracy with which I have been credited on this point, I have been largely requested, in writing this book, to give as many details as permissible. I shall endeavour to do so in as clear a way as possible, knowing well the difficulties that lie in the way of a lucid explanation of such a point.

In the first place, a thorough knowledge of all portions of the hand that can touch on this must be acquired. For instance, a person with a very poor development of the Mount of Venus is not so likely at any time to have children as the person with the mount full and large.

The lines relating to children are the fine upright lines from the end of the line of marriage. Sometimes these are so fine that it requires a microscope to make them out clearly, but in such a case it will be found that all the lines of the hand are also faint. By the position of these lines, by the portion of the mount they touch, by their appearance, and so on, one can accurately make out whether such children will play an important part in the life of the subject or otherwise; if they will be delicate or strong; if they will be male or female.

The leading points with regard to these lines are as follows:

Broad lines denote males; fine, narrow lines, females.

When they are clearly marked they denote strong, healthy children; when very faint, if they are wavy lines, they are the reverse.

When the first part of the line is a little island, the child will be very delicate in its early life, but if the line is well marked farther, it will eventually have good health.

When ending at the island, death will be the result.

When one line is longer and superior to the rest, one child will be more important to the parent than all the others.

The numbers run from the outside of the marriage-line in toward the hand.

On a man's hand they are often just as clear as on a woman's, but in such case the man will be exceptionally fond of children and will have an extremely affectionate nature; as a rule, however, the woman's hand shows the marks in a superior way. From these observations I think the student will be able to proceed in his or her pursuit of other minute details which I cannot go into here.

CHAPTER XVIII

THE STAR

THE star is a sign of very great importance, wherever it makes
its appearance on the hand. I do not at all hold that it is
generally a danger, and one from which there is no escape;
rather, on the contrary, I consider it, with one or two exceptions,
a fortunate sign, and one which naturally should depend upon
the portion of the hand, or the line, with which it is connected.

When a star appears on the Mount of Jupiter, it has two
distinct meanings, according to its position.

When on the highest point of the mount, on the face of the
hand, it promises great honour, power, and position; ambition
gratified, and the ultimate success and triumph of the individual
(Fig. 19, *m*).

With a strong fate-, head-, and sun-line, there is almost no
step in the ladder of human greatness that the subject will
not reach. It is usually found on the hand of a very ambitious
man or woman, and in the pursuit of power and position there
is probably no mark to equal it.

Its second position on the Mount of Jupiter is when it lies
almost off the mount, very low at its base, cutting the base of
the first finger, or resting on the side toward the back of the
hand. In this case it is also the sign of a most ambitious
person, but with this difference, that he will be brought in
contact with extremely distinguished people; but unless the
rest of the hand be exceptionally fine, it does not promise
distinction or power to the individual himself.

THE STAR ON THE MOUNT OF SATURN

On the centre of the Mount of Saturn it is a sign of some
terrible fatality (Fig. 19, *n*). It again gives distinction, but a
distinction to be dreaded. It is decidedly wrong to class this
sign with the old idea of the mark of murder. It really means

that the subject will have some terribly fatalistic life, but that of a man in every way a child of fate, a plaything of destiny; a man cast for some terrible part in the drama of life—he may be a Judas, or he may be a Saviour, but all his work and life and career will have some dramatic and terrible climax, some unrivalled brilliancy, some position resplendent with the majesty of death—a king for the moment, but crowned with doom.

The second position for the star on Saturn is that almost off the mount, either at the side or cutting into the fingers. This, like the star on Jupiter, denotes that the subject will be brought into contact with one of those who make history, but in this case with one who gains distinction through some terrible fate.

THE STAR ON THE MOUNT OF THE SUN

The star on the Mount of the Sun (Fig. 19, *p*) gives the brilliancy of wealth and position, but, as a rule, without happiness. Such wealth has come too late; the price has probably been too dearly paid in the way of health, or perhaps in peace of mind. Certain it is, however, that, though it gives great riches, it never gives contentment or happiness. When in this case by the side of the mount, it denotes, like the others, that the subject will be brought in contact with rich and wealthy people, without himself being rich in the world's goods.

When, however, it is connected or formed by the line of sun, it denotes great fame and celebrity, but through talent and work in art. It should not be too high on the hand; a little above the middle of the line is its best position, as in the case of Madame Sarah Bernhardt, an impression of whose hand will be found on Plate X.

THE STAR ON THE MOUNT OF MERCURY

The star in the centre of the Mount of Mercury (Fig. 19, *q*) denotes brilliancy and success in science, business, or the power of eloquence, according to the type of hand, and, as in the foregoing examples, by the side of the mount it denotes association with people distinguished in those walks of life.

THE STAR ON THE MOUNT OF MARS

The star on the Mount of Mars under Mercury (Fig. 18, *j*), denotes that through patience, resignation, and fortitude the greatest honours will be gained.

On the opposite side of the hand, the Mount of Mars under Jupiter, great distinction and celebrity will arise from a martial life, or a signal battle or warfare in which the subject will be engaged.

THE STAR ON THE MOUNT OF LUNA

The star on the Mount of Luna (Fig. 18, *k*) is, according to my system, a sign of great celebrity arising from the qualities of the mount, namely, through the imaginative faculties. I do not hold that it relates to drowning, in accordance with other cheiromants. There is another meaning, however, to this sign, which may have given rise to this idea, and that is that when the line of head ends in a star on this mount the dreamy imaginative faculties will ruin the balance of the line of head, and the result will be insanity. Because this star has been found so often on the hands of suicides, it may have given rise to the former belief, but people lose sight of the fact that water for suicides is going out of fashion. In these days the gas oven or an overdose of drug is much more in vogue.

THE STAR ON THE MOUNT OF VENUS

In the centre or highest point of the Mount of Venus (Fig. 18, *l*) the star is once more successful and favourable, but this time in relation to the affections and passions. On a man's hand such a sign indicates extraordinary success in all affairs of love—the same on a woman's hand. No jealousies or opposition will rob them of the spoils of conquest.

When lying by the side of the mount, the amours of such a subject will be with people distinguished for their success in the arena of love.

THE STAR ON THE FINGERS

The star on the tips or outer phalanges of the fingers gives great good fortune in anything touched or attempted, and on the first phalange of the thumb success through the subject's strength of will.

The star is one of the most important of the lesser signs to seek for.

In the foregoing remarks it should be borne in mind that the indications denoted by this important lesser sign must naturally be in keeping with the tendencies shown by the general character of the hand. It stands to reason, for instance, that the star could have little power or meaning on a hand containing a weak, undeveloped line of head. In dealing with this, as indeed with every other portion of the study, it must be understood that however clear the directions may be, it is impossible to dispense with the exercise of a certain amount of mentality and discretion on the part of the student.

CHAPTER XIX

THE CROSS

THE cross is the opposite to the star, and is seldom found as a favourable sign. It indicates trouble, disappointment, danger, and sometimes a change in the position or life, but one brought about by trouble. There is, however, one position in which it is a good sign to have it, namely, on the Mount of Jupiter (Fig. 18, *m*). In this position it indicates that at least one great affection will come into the life. This is especially the case when the line of fate rises from the Mount of Luna. A strange feature with this cross on Jupiter is that it denotes roughly about the time in life when the affection will influence the individual. When close to the commencement of the line of life and toward the side of the hand, it will be early; on the summit of the mount, in middle life; and down at the base, late in life.

On the Mount of Saturn (Fig. 18, *n*), when touching the line of fate, it denotes danger of violent death by accident; but when by itself in the centre of this mount, it increases the evil, fatalistic tendencies of the life.

On the Mount of the Sun it is a terrible sign of disappointment in the pursuit of fame, art, or riches.

The cross on the Mount of Mercury, as a rule, indicates a dishonest nature, and one inclined to duplicity.

On the Mount of Mars under Mercury it denotes the dangerous opposition of enemies; and on the Mount of Mars under Jupiter force, violence, and even death from quarrels.

A cross on the Mount of the Moon under the line of head denotes a fatal influence of the imagination. The man with such a sign will deceive even himself (Fig. 16, *l*).

On the Mount of Venus, when heavily marked, it indicates some great trial or fatal influence of affection; but when very small and lying close to the line of life, it tells of troubles and quarrels with near relatives.

A cross by the side of the line of fate, and between it and the life-line in the Plain of Mars, denotes opposition in one's career by relatives, and means a change in the destiny; but lying on the other side of the hand next to Luna it relates to a disappointment in a journey.

Above and touching the line of head, it fortells some wound or accident to the head.

By the side of the line of sun, disappointment in position.

Running into the line of fate, disappointment in money; and over the line of heart, the death of some loved one.

CHAPTER XX

THE SQUARE

THE square (Fig. 15) is one of the most interesting of the lesser signs. It is usually called "the mark of preservation," because it shows that the subject is protected at that particular point from whatever danger menaced.

When the line of fate runs through a well-formed square, it denotes one of the greatest crises in the subject's life in a worldly sense, connected with financial disaster or loss, but if the line goes right on through the square all danger will be averted. Even when the line of fate breaks in the centre, the square is still a sign of protection from very serious loss.

When outside the line, but only touching it, and directly under the Mount of Saturn, it denotes preservation from accident.

When the line of head runs through a well-formed square, it is a sign of strength and preservation to the brain itself, and tells of some terrible strain of work or of anxiety at that particular moment.

When rising above the line of head under Saturn, it foretells a preservation from some danger to the head.

When the line of heart runs through a square, it denotes some heavy trouble brought on by the affections. When under Saturn, some fatality to the object of one's affection (Fig. 21, *j*).

When the life-line passes through a square, it denotes a protection from death, even if the line be broken at that point (Fig. 21, *k*).

A square on the Mount of Venus inside the line of life denotes preservation from trouble brought on by the passions (Fig. 21, *l*). When resting in the centre of the Mount of Venus, it tells that the subject will fall into all kinds of danger through passion, but will always manage to escape.

When, however, lying outside the line of life and touching

it from the Plain of Mars, a square in such a place means imprisonment or seclusion from the world.

When on the mounts the square denotes a protection from any excess arising through the qualities of the mount:

On Jupiter, from the ambition of the subject.

On Saturn, from the fatality that shadows the life.

On the Sun, from the desire for fame.

On Mercury, from the restless, mercurial temperament.

On Mars, from danger through enemies.

On Luna, from an excess of imagination, or from the evil effects of some other line as, for instance, a line of travel.

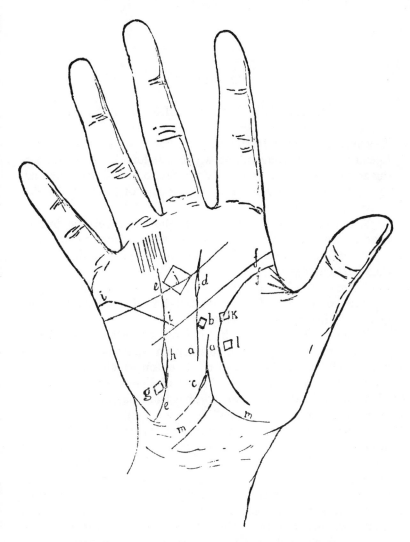

MODIFICATIONS OF THE PRINCIPAL LINES

Fig. 21

CHAPTER XXI

THE ISLAND, THE CIRCLE, THE SPOT

THE island is not a fortunate sign, but it only relates to the line or portion of the hand on which it is found. It is interesting to notice that it frequently relates to hereditary evils; as, for instance, heavily marked on the line of heart it denotes heart-disease inherited.

When as one distinct mark in the centre of the line of head, it denotes an hereditary weakness in relation to mentality.

When on the line of life, it denotes illness and delicacy at that particular point.

When on the line of fate, some heavy loss in worldly matters.

When on the line of sun, it foretells loss of position and name, generally through scandal (Fig. 21, *h*).

When on the line of health, it foreshadows a serious illness.

Any line running into or forming an island is a bad indication in relation to the part of the hand on which it is found.

An attendant line on the Mount of Venus running into an island foretells disgrace and trouble from passion to the man or woman who influences the life (Fig. 18, *p*).

A line forming an island and crossing the hand from the Mount of Venus to the line of marriage foretells that an evil influence at that particular point will cross the life and bring disgrace to the marriage (Fig. 18, *r*). If the same kind of line run to the line of heart, some bad influence will bring trouble and disgrace to the affections; when it runs to the line of head, some influence will direct the talents and intentions into some disgraceful channel; and when it runs into and bars the line of fate, some evil influence will be a barrier to the success of the subject at the date at which the lines join each other.

An island on any of the mounts injures the qualities of the mount on which it is found.

On the Mount of Jupiter it weakens the pride and ambition.

On Saturn it brings misfortune to the subject.

On the Mount of the Sun it weakens the talent for art.

On Mercury it makes a person too changeable to succeed, particularly in anything in relation to business or science.

On Mars it shows a weak spirit and cowardice.

On Luna, weakness in working out the power of the imagination.

On Venus, a person easily led and influenced by the sport of fancy and passion (Fig. 20, *k*).

THE CIRCLE

If found on the Mount of the Sun, the circle is a favourable mark. This is the only position in which it is fortunate. On any other mount it tells against the success of the subject.

On the Mount of Luna it denotes danger from drowning.

When touching any important line, it indicates that at that particular point the subject will not be able to clear himself from misfortune—in other words, he will, as it were, go round and round in a circle without being able to break through and get free.

THE SPOT

A spot is generally the sign of temporary illness.

A bright-red spot on the line of head indicates a shock or injury from some blow or fall.

A black or blue spot denotes a nervous illness.

A bright-red spot on the line of health is usually taken to mean fever, and on the line of life some illness of the nature of fever.

CHAPTER XXII

THE GRILLE, THE TRIANGLE, "LA CROIX MYSTIQUE," THE RING OF SOLOMON

THE grille (Fig. 15) is very often seen, and generally upon the mounts of the hand. It indicates obstacles against the success of that particular mount, and especially means that those obstacles are brought on by the tendencies of the subject in accordance with that portion of the hand in which it is found.

On the Mount of Jupiter it denotes egotism, pride, and the dominative spirit.

On the Mount of Saturn it foretells misfortune, a melancholy nature, and a morbid tendency.

On the Mount of the Sun it tells of vanity, folly, and a desire for celebrity.

On the Mount of Mercury it denotes an unstable and rather unprincipled person.

On the Mount of Luna it foretells restlessness, discontent, and disquietude.

On the Mount of Venus, caprice in passion.

THE TRIANGLE

The triangle (Fig. 15) is a curious sign, and is often found clear and distinct, and not formed by the chance crossing of lines.

When distinct in shape on the Mount of Jupiter, it promises more than usual success in the management of people, in the handling of men, and even in the organization of everyday affairs.

On the Mount of Saturn it gives a talent and inclination for mystical work, for the delving into the occult, for the study of human magnetism, and so forth.

On the Mount of the Sun it denotes a practical application

of art and a calm demeanour toward success and fame.   Success will never spoil such people.

On the Mount of Mercury it checks its restless qualities, and promises success in relation to business or money.

On the Mount of Mars, it gives science in warfare, great calmness in any crisis, and presence of mind in danger.

On the Mount of Luna it tells of a scientific method in following out the ideas of the imagination.

On the Mount of Venus, calmness and calculation in love, the power of restraint and control over self.

The tripod or spear-head (Fig. 15) is an excellent sign of success on any mount on which it is found.

"LA CROIX MYSTIQUE"

This strange mark has usually for its domain the centre of the quadrangle (Fig. 19, *r*), but it may be found at either its upper or lower extremities.   It may be formed by the line of fate and a line from the head to the heart, or it may lie as a distinct mark without connection with any other main line.

It denotes mysticism, occultism, and superstition.

These three qualities are widely apart in themselves, although often confounded, and the position this mark takes on the hand is therefore very important.

When high up on the hand toward Jupiter, it will give the belief in mysticism for one's own life, but not the desire to follow it farther than where it relates to self.   Such people want their fortunes told, actuated more by curiosity to know how their own ambitions will turn out than by the deeper interest that the study involves for its own sake.

When the "Croix Mystique" is more closely connected with the line of heart than with that of head, it gives a superstitious nature, and this even more so when it is marked over the centre of the head-line, when that line takes a sharp curve downward. It must be remembered that the length of the line of head has much to do with this.   The very short line with the cross over it will be a thousand times more superstitious than the long one.   The long one will be the greatest for occultism, and particularly so if the "Croix Mystique" is an independent formation on the line of head.

When it touches the fate-line, or is formed by it, the love of the mystic will influence the entire career.

THE RING OF SOLOMON

The Ring of Solomon (Fig. 12) is a sign that also denotes the love of the occult, but in this case it shows more the power of the master, the adept, than the mere love of the mystic denoted by "La Croix Mystique."

CHAPTER XXIII

HANDS COVERED WITH LINES—THE COLOUR OF THE PALM

WHEN the entire hand is covered with a multitude of fine lines like a net spreading over its surface, it tells that the nature is intensely nervous and sensitive, but one that will be continually disturbed and worried by little thoughts and troubles that would be of no importance whatever to others.

This is particularly so if the palm be soft—such people imagine all sorts of things in the way of ailments and troubles; but if the palm of the hand be hard and firm, it denotes an energetic, excitable nature, but one that is far more successful for other people than for self.

SMOOTH HANDS

Very smooth hands with few lines belong to people calm in temperament and even in disposition. They seldom if ever worry; they rarely lose temper, but when they do they know the reason why. This is again modified by the palm being hard or soft. When firm, it is a greater sign of control and calmness than when soft. In the latter case it is not so much a matter of control as of indifference: the subject will not take sufficient interest to lose temper—that would be too much of an exertion.

THE SKIN

When the palm of the hand is covered naturally with a very fine light skin, the subject will retain the buoyancy and temperament of youth much longer than the person with a coarse skin. This is, of course, much affected by work, but I am speaking of cases where little labour or manual work is done; yet even where there is manual work this can still be observed by the ridges of the skin.   It has been proved that even as regards this point no two hands are ever alike; consequently, while work may thicken the cuticle, its individuality remains the same.

THE COLOUR OF THE PALM

The colour of the palm is far more important than the colour of the outside of the hands.   This at first sight appears strange, but a little observation will prove its truth.

The palm of the hand is under the immediate control and action of the nerves and of the nerve-fluid.   According to scientists, there are more nerves in the hand than in any other portion of the body, and, again, more in the palm than in any other portion of the hand.   As regards the nerve-fluid, Abercrombie, in his work published in London in 1838, states that "the communication of preception from the senses to the mind has been accounted for by the motions of the nervous fluids, a subtle essence resembling electricity or galvanism." It therefore follows that this subtle essence must affect the palm more than any other portion of the body.   There is every reason, therefore, why the colour of the palm should be of more importance than that of the back of the hand.

It will be found that almost every palm has a distinct colour and can be classed as follows:

When pale or almost white in colour, the subject will take very little interest in anything outside of himself—in other words, he will be selfish, egotistical, and unsympathetic.

When the palm is yellowish in colour, the subject will be morbid, melancholy, and morose.

When a delicate pink, the nature is sanguine, hopeful, and bright; and when very red, robust in health and spirits, passionate, and quick-tempered.

CHAPTER XXIV

THE GREAT TRIANGLE AND THE QUADRANGLE

WHAT is called the great triangle, or the Triangle of Mars, is
formed by the lines of life, head, and the hepatica (Fig. 22).

When, as is very frequently the case, the line of health is
altogether absent, its place must be filled by an imaginary line
to form the base of the triangle, or (as is often found) the line
of sun forms the base (Fig. 22, *a–a*). This latter is by far the
greatest sign of power and success, although the subject will
not be so broad-minded and liberal as when the base of the
triangle is formed by the line of health.

The shape and positions of the great triangle must be considered by themselves, although it contains the upper, the
middle, and the lower angle, which three points will be dealt
with later.

When the triangle is well formed by the lines of head, life,
and health, it should be broad and enclose the entire Plain of
Mars. In such case it denotes breadth of views, liberality and
generosity of spirit; such a person will be inclined to sacrifice
himself to further the interests of the whole, not the unit.

If, on the contrary, it is formed by three small, wavy, uncertain lines, it denotes timidity of spirit, meanness, and cowardice.
Such a man would always go with the majority, even against
his principles.

When in the second formation of the triangle it has for its
base the line of sun, the subject will then have narrow ideas
but great individuality and strong resolution. Such a sign,
from the very qualities it exhibits, contains within itself the
seeds of worldly success.

THE UPPER ANGLE

The upper angle (Fig. 22, *b*) is formed by the lines of head
and life. This angle should be clear, well pointed, and even.

Such will indicate refinement of thought and mind, and delicacy toward others.

When very obtuse, it denotes a dull matter-of-fact intellect with little delicacy and feeling and a very small appreciation of art or of artistic things or people.

When extremely wide and obtuse, it gives a blunt, hasty temper, a person who will continually offend people. It also denotes impatience and want of application in study.

THE MIDDLE ANGLE

The middle angle is formed by the line of head and that of health (Fig. 22, c). If clear and well defined, it denotes quickness of intellect, vivacity, and good health.

When very acute, it denotes a painfully nervous temperament and bad health.

When very obtuse, dullness of intelligence and a matter-of-fact method of working.

THE LOWER ANGLE

The lower angle (Fig. 22, d), when very acute and made by the hepatica, denotes feebleness, and littleness of spirit; when obtuse, it denotes a strong nature.

When made by the line of sun and very acute, it gives individuality, but a narrow view of things; when obtuse, it gives a broader and more generous mind.

THE QUADRANGLE

The quadrangle, as its name implies, is that quadrangular space between the lines of head and heart (Fig. 22).

It should be even in shape, wide at both ends, but not narrow at the centre. Its interior should be smooth and not crossed with many lines, whether from the head or from the heart. When marked in this way, it indicates evenness of mind, power of intellect and loyalty in friendship or affection.

This space represents within itself the man's disposition toward his fellows. When excessively narrow, it shows narrow ideas, smallness of thought, and bigotry, but more in

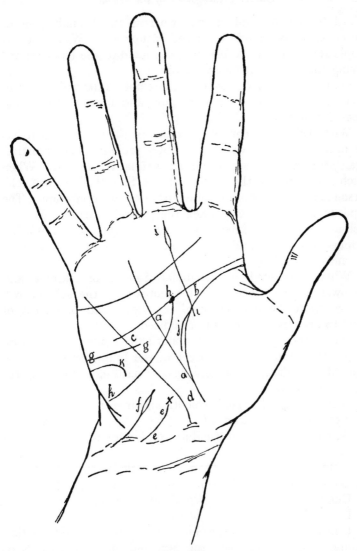

MODIFICATIONS OF THE PRINCIPAL LINE⹁

Fig. 22

regard to religion and morals, whereas the triangle denotes conservatism as regards work and occupation.   With religious people this is a remarkable sign, the hand of the bigot always having this space extremely narrow.

On the other hand, the space must not be too wide.   When it is, the subject's views of religion and morals will be too broad for his own good.

When this space narrows so much in the centre that it has the appearance of a waist, it denotes prejudice and injustice. Again, the two ends should be fairly equally balanced.   When much wider under the Mount of the Sun than Saturn, the person is careless about his name, position, or reputation.   The opposite of this is shewn when the space is narrow.   It is in such a case a sign of intense anxiety as to the opinion of other people—what the world thinks, and what one must do to keep up one's reputation.

When excessively wide under Saturn or Jupiter and narrower at the other end, it denotes that the subject will change from the generosity of his views and broadness of mind to become narrow and prejudiced.

When the quadrangle is abnormally wide in its entire length, it denotes want of order in the brain, carelessness of thought and ideas, an unconventional nature, and one imprudent in every way.

When the quadrangle is smooth and free from little lines, it denotes a calm temperament.

When very full of little lines and crosses, the nature is restless and irritable.

A star in any portion of the quadrangle is an excellent sign, particularly if it be under some favourable mount.

Under Jupiter it promises pride and power.

Under Saturn, success in worldly matters.

Under the Mount of the Sun, success in fame and position through art; and between the Sun and Mercury, success in science and research.

CHAPTER XXV

TRAVEL, VOYAGES, AND ACCIDENTS

THERE are two distinct ways of telling travels and voyages. One is from the heavy lines on the face of the Mount of Luna; the other, from the little hair-lines that leave the line of life but travel on with it (Fig. 22, *j*). This indication is similar to that of the line of life dividing in the hand: if one branch goes around Venus, the other proceeding to the base of the Mount of Luna, it foretells that the subject will make some great change from his native land to another. It therefore follows that the journeys told by the change in the line of life are far more important than the lines on Luna, which relate more to the minor changes or travels of the subject. It is sometimes found that long lines extend from the *rascette*, or first bracelet (Fig. 22), and rise into the Mount of Luna. These are similar to the travel-lines on Luna, but much more important. When the line of fate shows a considerable and beneficial change at the same point, then these lines are prosperous and fortunate. When, however, the line of fate does not show any advantage gained at the same point, the subject will not improve, to any great extent, in worldly matters by the change.

When such a journey-line ends with a small cross, the journey will end in disappointment (Fig. 22, *e–e*).

When the travel-line ends in a square, it denotes danger from the journey, but the subject will be protected.

When the line ends with an island, no matter how small, the journey will result in loss (Fig. 22, *f*).

On the Mount of Luna the ascendant lines from the *rascette* are the most beneficial.

When the line crosses the hand and enters the Mount of Jupiter, great position and power will be gained by it, and the journey will also be extremely long.

When the travel-line runs to the Mount of Saturn, some fatality will govern the entire journey

When it runs to the Mount of the Sun, it is most favourable, and promises riches and fame.

When it reaches the Mount of Mercury, sudden and unexpected wealth will arise from it.

When the horizontal lines on Luna cross the face of the mount and reach the line of fate, the journeys will be longer and more important than those indicated by the short, heavy lines also on that mount, though they may not relate to a change of country (Fig. 22, g–g).

When they enter the line of fate and ascend with it, they denote travels that will materially benefit the subject.

When the end of any of these horizontal lines droop or curve downward toward the wrist, the journey will be unfortunate (Fig. 22, k). When they rise upward, no matter how short, it will be successful.

When one of these lines crosses another, such a journey will be repeated, but for some important reason.

Any square on such a line will show danger, but protection from accident or misfortune.

If the travel-line runs into the line of head and causes a spot, island, or break, it foretells some danger to the head, or some malady arising from such a journey (Fig. 22, h–h).

ACCIDENTS

I have alluded to accidents considerably in my treatment of the line of travel and in relation to travel, but disasters are more marked on the line of life and line of head than at any other point.

In the first place, the accident marked to the line of life denotes a more immediate danger of death, as follows:

When, from an island on Saturn, a line falls downward and enters the life-line, serious, if not fatal, danger is indicated (Fig. 22, i–i).

When such a line ends by a small cross, either on the line of life or without it, it tells that the subject will have some narrow escape from serious accident.

When the same mark occurs lower down, at the base of the Mount of Saturn, the accident will result more from animals than from other causes.

Any straight line from Saturn to the life-line means danger of some kind, but not so serious as from a line possessing the island either on Saturn or lower down.

To the line of head exactly the same rules apply, with this difference, that the danger will be direct to the head itself, but unless the accident-line cut or break the head-line the danger does not signify death as much as when marked on the line of life: it denotes, as it were, that the person has time to foresee the dangers that approach, and such a mark indicates a fright and shock to the brain, but no serious results unless the line is injured or broken.

CHAPTER XXVI

TIME—THE SYSTEM OF SEVEN

In my own work I use a system as regards time and dates which I have never found mentioned elsewhere. It is one which I consider exceptionally accurate, and I therefore recommend it to the student for his or her consideration. It is the system of seven, and I advance it as being taught by nature in all her mysterious dealings with life.

In the first place, we find from a medical and scientific standpoint the seven a most important point of calculation. We find that the entire system undergoes a complete change every seven years; that there are seven stages of the prenatal existence; that the brain takes seven forms before it takes upon itself "the unique character of the human brain"; and so forth. Again, we find that in all ages the number seven has played a most important part in the history of the world; as, for instance, the seven races of humanity, the seven wonders of the world, the seven altars to the seven gods of the seven planets, the seven days of the week, the seven colours, the seven minerals, the supposition of the seven senses, the three parts of the body each containing seven sections, and the seven divisions of the world. Again, in the Bible seven is the most important number; but it is superfluous to give further details. The point that bears most largely on this subject is that of the entire system undergoing a change every seven years. My own observation leads me also to advance (simply for the consideration of the student) the theory that the alternate sevens are somewhat alike in their relation to the functional changes of the body. For example, a child very delicate on passing the age of seven is also likely to be delicate on passing the age of twenty-one, whereas a child healthy and strong at the age of seven will again be healthy and strong at twenty-one, no matter how delicate he or she may be through the intermediate years. This is an interesting point in predictions

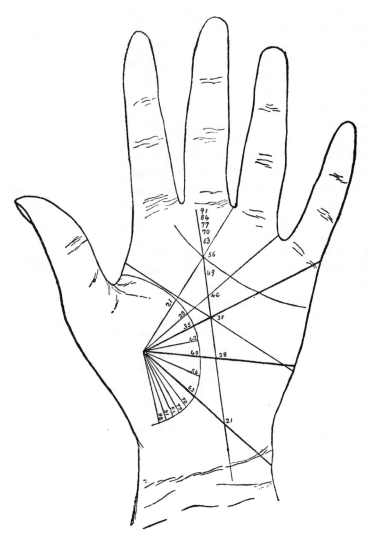

TIME—THE SYSTEM OF SEVEN

Fig. 23

relating to health, and one which I have found not only interesting but extremely reliable. Every line on the hand can be
divided into sections giving dates with more or less accuracy.
The most important lines, however, and those usually consulted
in reference to dates, are those of life and fate. In Fig. 23 it
will be noticed that I have divided the line of fate into three
great divisions, namely, twenty-one, thirty-five, and forty-
nine, and if the student will keep this in mind he will more
easily fill in the subdivisions on the human hand itself. The
point, however, which I cannot impress too strongly, is that
the student must notice the class or type of hand before proceeding or attempting to make the smallest calculation. It stands
to reason that there must be the greatest difference between the
dates given by the palm of the square or spatulate hand and
that of the psychic. If the student will bear this in mind, he
will reduce or increase his scale in accordance with the length
of the palm. Mentally to divide the lines into sections as illustrated will be found the simplest and the most accurate plan
that the student can pursue.

When, in the calculation of dates, the line of life and the
line of fate are used together, it will be found that they corro-
borate one another and give accuracy as to the events. It is
therefore not difficult, after a little practice, to give a date as
to when an illness or an event took place, or when such and
such a thing will happen. Practice gives perfection in all
things; let not the student be discouraged, therefore, if at first
he finds difficulty in dividing the lines into divisions and subdivisions.

PART III: ILLUSTRATIVE TYPES

CHAPTER I

A FEW WORDS ON SUICIDE

I WILL now deal with a few illustrative types to help the student in the congregation of lines, signs, and formations that go to form each individual character. It is seldom, if ever, that one distinct mark or peculiarity has the power to ruin or blight any one nature. An evil or dangerous sign as regards character merely shows the particular tendency in this or that direction. It takes a variety of wheels to make a watch: so does it take a variety of characteristics to make a criminal or a saint. The type bearing the disposition toward suicide is a very striking example of this. But before I go farther I would like to make a few remarks as to the subject of suicide itself. In every town in which I may reside, an establishment which has considerable interest for me is that strange temple of death, the morgue. Why not? If one in any sense studies life, he should study it to the borders of that "undiscovered country, from whose bourn no traveller returns." The semi-barbarous, semi-human idea that by such an act the suicide has made him or herself an outcast, not only to this world, but to the next, cannot be too highly condemned. Even in this so-called enlightened age I have seen clergymen refuse to attend the grave. In some countries I have seen the body of the suicide dug up in the dead of night and buried in the sand of the sea-shore, or, worse still, thrown over the cliffs into the sea. It is not the treatment of the corpse against which I raise my voice—the dead feel nothing, the corpse is clay—it is the brutality of the living that makes me speak.

I must lay considerable stress on this point of suicide, even if I am severely criticized for my remarks—for what would be the good of attempting to analyse life if one did not state his opinions freely and without reserve? I know I shall be criticized for saying that I have not found that it is weak-minded people who generally commit suicide. On the contrary, I have merely found that they belong to a different class of mentality from those who prefer to hang on to the skirts of life through misery and misfortune. It is preposterous that we should set up any narrow lines of what is right or what is wrong, knowing as we do that we are, and always have been, in complete ignorance of the laws governing life, from the birth of the child to the development of the individual. What seems right to one may be utterly wrong to another, according to the mental vision which decides our conduct. There is a well-known disease which affects the senses in such a way that the scratching of a pencil in the same room sounds to the sufferer like the rumble of a mail-cart, while the striking of a match seems more dazzling than a flash of lightning. In the same way the mind, under pressure of desire, of sorrow, or of anxiety, may become more keenly sensitive to "the slings and arrows of outrageous fortune." Why, then, should we judge and measure and condemn such people, simply because we do not all see with their eyes, hear with their ears, and understand with their understanding?

I must also take exception to the everyday phrase of the jury—"Committed suicide while the balance of his mind was disturbed," as used in reference to all people, whether evidence is given to prove insanity or not. The idea that because an individual commits suicide he must necessarily be insane, is on the face of it absurd, as it has often been demonstrated that the most marvellous reason and logic have been used to balance every side of the question before the individual has come to the conclusion that in his particular case the search for death was the noblest thing in life. I have known suicides to show the greatest possible courage, the strongest fortitude, and the greatest will in facing that mighty angel of mystery whom, all their life long, they have been taught to avoid and dread. I have known the most noble deeds of silent martyrdom performed by those who afterward would scarce receive Christian burial. I have known not a few cases of persons suffering from an incurable disease ending life a few months sooner—and why? Not because of the agony they suffered, but because they were causing their children to suffer, and burdening them with expenditure which they could not afford; and yet I have been told that such a person could have no part or lot in that kingdom of peace, be it rest or be it life, which lies beyond the silence of the tomb. Is it man, or ghoul, or devil, I ask, who has thus the presumption to dictate to man the wishes or the judgments of that which is Almighty? What man among the mortals of the earth has the right to elect himself the mouth-piece of the Omnipotent and the Unknown? How many poor suicides has this relic of barbarianism condemned to the ever-lasting torment of the spirit? How many mothers has this fetishism broken beneath the wheels of its Juggernaut? How many sisters have cried and sobbed beneath the darkness of the night? How many brothers have raised defiant eyes to heaven that such a thing could be?

Alas! thou great Spirit of life, of death, of all that is, of all that will be, we know not thy name, thy being, thy creation, or the ultimate purpose for which thou hast endowed man and shaped man in the carrying out of thy design. As we are nothing, forgive us all things; as we ask for nothing, give us but what we need; and as we be nothing, be thou to us the all-sufficient, the life, the death, the eternal of the soul.

CHAPTER II

THE PECULIARITIES OF HANDS WHICH SHOW A SUICIDAL TENDENCY

THE hand is generally long, with a sloping line of head, and a developed Mount of Luna, particularly toward its base. The line of head is also very much connected with the line of life, and so increases the excessively sensitive nature of the subject. In such a case the individual would not naturally be morbid or even show the inclination for suicide, but the nature is so sensitive and so imaginative that any trouble, grief, or scandal is intensified a thousandfold, and to kill or injure self gives the peculiar satisfaction of self-martyrdom to such a type, as exemplified by Plate XV.

The same indications being found in connection with a well-developed Mount of Saturn, will give the thoroughly sensitive morbid nature; an individual who will determinedly come to the conclusion that life under any circumstances is not worth living—so the slightest provocation by trouble or disappointment causes him quietly and resignedly to fly to that last resource which he has cherished and thought of for so long.

The excessively drooping line of head (Plate XV) on a pointed or conic hand denotes the same result, but only through the sudden impulse that is characteristic of the nature. To such a person a shock or trouble is all-sufficient to impart the impulse to the excitable disposition, and before there is time to think, the deed is done.

The opposite of this excitability is shown in the case of the subject's committing suicide when the line of head is not abnormally sloping. Such a person, however, will have the line closely connected with the line of life, a depressed Mount of Jupiter, and a very fully-developed Saturn. Such a subject will feel the disappointments of life unusually keenly; he will as well have a melancholy and gloomy turn of mind; he will, however, be logical in weighing every side of the question for life and death, and if he arrives at the conclusion that the game is up and the battle over as far as he is concerned, he will, in a most reasonable and sensible manner, according to his standpoint, proceed to put an end to all misfortunes. What such a person will suffer before he arrives at this conclusion it is scarcely possible to estimate. We are all so wrapped up in our own interests and affairs that we hardly see or notice the pale, worn face that has suffered so patiently, the hollow eyes of wakeful nights, the wasted cheeks of hunger, which appear for a moment by our side, and are gone for ever.

PROPENSITIES FOR MURDER

MURDER can be divided into a great many different classes. What the hand principally recognizes is that of the abnormal tendency toward crime, the class of crime itself being traced by the type of hand in respect to the inclinations of the subject. That some people have a natural predilection toward murder cannot, I think, be doubted. There are born criminals as well as born saints. It depends upon the development of the will, in keeping with the surroundings and circumstances, whether the criminal tendencies will be developed or not. The destructive tendency as exhibited by children does not denote their want of sense, but denotes the innate sense of destruction before it has been curbed by the fear of consequences, by the will, or the surroundings that are brought to bear upon the nature. Some people born into the world have this propensity more developed than others; the slightest flaw in their surroundings being responsible for the after-evolution of the criminal. Again, I do not hold that to be criminal in giving way to passion, to temptation, is to be weak-minded. On the contrary, crime can only be considered in relation to the individual. What is temptation to one is not temptation to another. I do not hold that because of such things crime should go unpunished; on the contrary, crime must be dealt with for the protection of the community: but what I do hold is, that crime should be punished in accordance with the individual and not in accordance with the crime.

It therefore follows that in the study of crime one must place one's self as far as possible in the position of the criminal. (It is astonishing how many different expressions one finds in the face of a picture from different points of view.)

As regards the hand, it divides murder into three very distinct classes:

1.   The murderer made so by the instinct to kill, as exhibited in the brute creation, through passion, fury, or revenge.

2.   The murderer made so by the greed of gain; the nature that will stop at nothing in order to gratify its covetous tendency.

3.   The utterly heartless disposition which feeds on the sufferings of others; the nature that will even live on friendly terms with the victim—the one that will, as it were, deal out death in drops of honey; the person who cannot be touched by the longings for life exhibited by the sufferer, and who, though keenly alive to the danger, feels in that danger a sense of delight, and, with utter lack of moral consciousness, takes more pleasure in such work than in the gain it brings.

The first class is very ordinary.   The man or woman becomes a murderer by circumstances.   Such an individual may be thoroughly good-natured and kind-hearted, but some provocation excites the blind fury of the animal nature, and when the deed is done, such a one is generally crushed and broken by remorse.

In such cases the hand shows no bad sign more than ungovernable temper and brute passion.   It is, in fact, the elementary hand, or a near approach to it.   The line of head is short, thick, and red, the nails short and red, and the hand heavy and coarse.   The most remarkable characteristic, however, will be the thumb.   The thumb will be set very low on the hand; it will be short and thick in the second phalange, and the first phalange will be what is called "the clubbed thumb" (Fig. 8), very short, broad, and square: this is found almost without exception in such types.   If in such cases the Mount of Venus is also abnormally large, sexual passion will be the destroyer; when not unusually developed, the greatest failing will be that of ungovernable temper.

In the second class none of these points will be abnormal; the most striking peculiarity will be the line of head, which will be heavily marked, but with a decided growth upward (Plate XIV); it will be found in an abnormal position, rising high toward Mercury, or far before it reaches that point it completely leaves its place on the right hand; as the propensities become stronger, it enters the line of heart, takes possession of it, as it were, and thus completely masks all the generous impulses or kind thoughts of the subject. (See previous remarks on the line of head, Part II, Chapter IX, page 131.) The hand is usually hard, the thumb not abnormally thick, but long, very stiff, and contracted inward. The entire formation gives covetous propensities, and an utter want of conscience in the pursuit of gain.

The third class, to the student of human nature, is the most interesting, though it may be the most terrible.

It is the hand of the subtlest nature in regard to crime. There will be nothing abnormal in connection with the hand itself. It will be only by examination of all the characteristics that the treacherous side of this nature will be discovered. The leading features, however, will be a very thin, hard hand, long, the fingers generally slightly curved inward; the thumb long, and with both phalanges well developed, giving both the ability to plan and the strength of will necessary for execution; it will rarely, if ever, be found bent or inclining outward, although such a formation exists at times on the hands of the first-mentioned class.

The line of head may or may not be out of its proper position. It will, however, be set higher than usual across the hand, but will be very long and very thin, denoting the treacherous instincts. The Mount of Venus may be either depressed on the hand, or very high. When depressed, such a subject will commit crime simply for the sake of crime; when high, the crime will be committed more for the sake of satisfying the animal desires.

Such are the hands of the skilled artists in crime. Murder with such persons is reduced to a fine art, in the execution of which they will study every detail. They will rarely, if ever, kill their victim by violence—such a thing would be vulgar in their eyes—poison is the chief instrument that they employ, but so skilfully that the verdict is usually "Death from natural causes."

VARIOUS PHASES OF INSANITY

It has often been said that all men are mad on some particular point. It is when this madness passes the half-way point of eccentricity that the title "lunatic" is bestowed upon the individual. As there are many forms of madness, so are there many indications given by the hand. The chief types which we will consider here are the following:

1. Melancholy and religious madness, hallucinations, etc.
2. The development of the crank.
3. The natural madman.

MELANCHOLY AND RELIGIOUS MADNESS

In the first case the line of head, on a rather broad hand, descends with a sharp curve low down on the Mount of Luna, very often to the base, denoting the abnormally imaginative temperament of the subject. In addition to this, the Mount of Venus is not well developed, thus decreasing the subject's interest in all human or natural things; and lastly, the Mount of Saturn dominates.

As a rule, such is the hand of the religious maniac. He commences early in life with strong hallucinations from the extraordinary imagination that he possesses, which imagination, if directed into the proper channel, would probably work off its excess and relieve itself, but if opposed, feeds on itself, and thus increases. At first this is shown only occasionally in fits and starts. Its periods then grow longer and longer, until at last its moments of balance are few and far between. This is the morbid or melancholy type of the religious maniac.

THE DEVELOPMENT OF THE CRANK

This type of madness is generally found in conjunction with two very distinct types—the spatulate and the philosophic.

In the first type it is the very sloping line of head on an extremely spatulate formation. At the commencement it merely denotes daring originality, which will show itself in every possible direction. It dissipates its own power by attempting too many things, owing to the multitude of its inventive ideas. Again I say, if the subject could only get into some position in life where he might work off those ideas, all would be well, and he might even give to the world some great invention or discovery which would benefit mankind. But attempt to crush such a man by some occupation entirely foreign to his nature, and you instantly turn all his current of thought to some extraordinary invention which he attempts to work out in secret; one which he dreams will be successful, and whose success will emancipate him from the slavery he is under. The very fact of his having to work in secret, the weakening of his nerve-power by confinement and by intensity of thought, the excitement under which he labours, is the laboratory where, in the end, he turns himself out—mad.

The next type is the philosophic. This is again shown by a sudden curve of the line of head on the Mount of Luna, and with an accentuated philosophic formation. In this case the crank, and eventually the madman, leans toward the extraordinary in the salvation of mankind. He means well, from first to last; he is, however, a fanatic on whatever point, doctrine, or theory he advances. It requires but unfavourable circumstances, non-success, and the indifference of the public to make this subject pass the half-way mark of eccentricity and become the lunatic.

If his weak point be religion, his is never that of the melancholy; on the contrary, he is the only person who knows the secret of the kingdom of heaven—all others are lost. It is not that he wishes to be alone when he gets there—it is his feverish anxiety for others which makes him exceptional. For this object he works day and night; he denies himself the enjoyment of life, even food, in the terrible haste to accomplish his desire; the brain becomes more and more off its balance, and the man becomes more and more mad.

THE NATURAL MADMAN

Malformation of the brain is responsible for this type, which, by a study of the hand, can be divided into two distinct classes—that of the hopeless idiot, and that of the vicious lunatic.

In the first class we generally find a wide, sloping line of head, formed entirely of islands and little hair-lines. This never gives any hope whatever of reason or intelligence, and denotes that the subject has been brought into the world with a brain insufficient—either in quantity or in quality—to govern or control the body, and the hopeless idiot is the result.

In the second division of this type the line of head, instead of being a continuous line, is made up of short, wavy branches running in all directions. A number of them rise inside the line of life on Mars, and cross to the other Mars on the opposite side of the hand. With this formation the nails are generally short and red. Such a type denotes the quarrelsome, vicious lunatic more than any other class. In this case it will be noted that there are often sane moments, but such are extremely rare, and with regard to the last two classes I have never known any recovery.

CHAPTER V

MODUS OPERANDI

IN the first place, I would advise the student to seat himself opposite his subject, so that a good light may fall directly on the hands. I would also advise that no person be allowed to stand or sit in close proximity, as unconsciously a third person will distract the attention of both subject and palmist. There is no special time absolutely necessary for the successful reading of hands. In India they advocate the hour of sunrise, but that is merely because of the fact that the circulation of the blood is stronger at the extremities in the early morning, than after the fatigue of the day, consequently the lines are more coloured and distinct. By placing the subject directly opposite, the student is in a better position to examine both hands at the same time. In proceeding with the examination, first notice carefully the type the hands belong to, whether the fingers are in keeping with the palm, or in themselves relate to a distinct class; next carefully examine the left hand, then turn to the right—see what modifications and changes have occurred there, and make the right hand the basis of your reading.

On all important points, such as illness, death, loss of fortune, marriage, and so forth, see what the left promises before coming to the conclusion that this or that event will take place.

Hold whatever hand you are examining firmly in yours; press the line or mark till the blood flows into it—you will see by this means the tendencies of its growth.

Examine every portion of the hand—back, front, nails, skin, colour—before speaking. The first point should be the examination of the thumb; see whether it is long, short, or poorly developed; whether the will-phalange is firm or supple, whether it is strong or weak. Then turn your attention to the palm: note whether it is hard, soft or flabby.

196

I would next advise that you remark the fingers—their proportion to the palm, whether long or short, thick or thin; class them as a whole, according to the type they represent, or if they be mixed, class each individual finger. Then notice the nails, for their bearing on temper, disposition, and health. Finally, after carefully examining the entire hand, turn your attention to the mounts: see which mount or mounts have the greatest prominence; and then proceed to the lines. There is no fixed rule as to the line to examine first; the best plan, however, is to start with the lines of life and health combined, then proceed to the line of head, the line of destiny, the line of heart, and so on.

Speak honestly, truthfully, yet carefully. You can tell the plainest truths, but you need not shock or hurt your consultant by doing so. Be as careful with that complicated piece of humanity before you as you would be in handling a fine and delicate piece of machinery. Above all things, you must be sympathetic: take the deepest possible interest in every person whose hands you read; enter into their lives, their feelings, and their natures. Let your entire ambition be to do good, to be of some benefit to the person who consults you. If this be the foundation of your work, it will never tire or distress you; on the contrary, it will sustain you. If you meet friends, be thankful for their friendliness; if you meet enemies, be not argumentative for the sake of argument. Think of your work first, of self last.

Above all things, be not impatient in the pursuit of this knowledge; you will not learn a language in a day, neither must you expect to learn cheiromancy in an hour. Be not dismayed if you find it more difficult than you have imagined. Consider it earnestly—not in the light of an amusement, but as a work entailing depth of thought, patience of research, and one worthy of the highest talents that you can give. If we study it aright, we hold within our hands the keys of the mysteries of life. In it are hereditary laws, the sins of the fathers, the karma of the past, the effect of the cause, the balance of things that have been, the shadow of things to be.

Let us be careful, then, that this knowledge be used aright. Let us be earnest in work, humble if success may crown work. Let us examine self before we examine others. If we see crime, let us consider the temptation of the criminal. If we see faults, let us remember we are not perfect.

Let us be careful lest in the pursuit of knowledge we despise what may seem to be beneath us—there is nothing beneath us; there is nothing common, for all fulfil the purpose of humanity. Let us not think there is no truth because we do not know, or that we possess the mysteries of the sun because we see its light. Let us be humble, that knowledge may raise us; let us be seekers, that we may find.

PART IV

THE APPARATUS FOR "THOUGHT PHOTOGRAPHY AND REGISTER OF CEREBRAL FORCE"

IN the earlier pages of this work it will be noticed that I have alluded more than once to the idea of the brain generating an unknown force, which not only, by its radiations through the body, caused marks and variations on and in the body, but that also through the medium of the ether in the atmosphere every human being was more or less in touch with and influenced by one another (see pages 35, 37, and 40).

When I first made this statement years ago, I did not do so only on an opinion based on the writings of scientists such as Abercrombie, Herder, and others, for I had at that time a tangible proof that such a force did exist through experiments made by my friend, the well-known French *savant*, Monsieur E. Savary d'Odiardi. I knew some years before I wrote of this force that this gentleman had invented an apparatus which had been exhibited before the Académie des Sciences, Paris, in which a needle of metal could be moved a distance of ten degrees by a person of strong will concentrating his attention on it at a distance of from two to three feet.

This little machine was in its infancy, and although scientists marvelled at it, yet there were few who thought it would ever be so far perfected as to be of use in any practical way; but the brain of the man who could think out and invent such an apparatus could not be satisfied to rest at such small beginnings; for nearly five years he patiently worked and laboured on, until at last, after many setbacks, he triumphed over all obstacles, and constructed an apparatus which completely eclipsed the first machine he had invented, and showed with *every person* the action of thought in the brain, and which, instead of being able to move only ten degrees, could register 360 in one movement. From that time on he confined his attentions to observations of the registering needle with people of different emotions and idiosyncrasies of temperament.

In his electro-medical hospital for the cure of diseases reputed incurable by ordinary means, he had ample opportunities for watching the effect of various temperaments and diseases on this singular apparatus. The result of his work was to enable him, by "the observation of cases," to make certain rules to act as a guide in watching the indications of this instrument.

Subsequently, I had the honour of assisting Professor d'Odiardi with various experiments in connection with this apparatus; and finally, for the sake of obtaining charts of all sorts and conditions of people, he requested me to collaborate with him in the use of this machine, in order that he might enlarge his scope and field of observation.

After placing notes made from hundreds of experiments in my hands, I took the instrument to my rooms in Bond Street, and tested it upward of thirty to forty times a day in connection with the various people who visited me.

The proof that the needle in this machine was influenced by a force radiating from the brain was shewn by the Professor in his experiments with people who approached it under the influence of certain drugs that injure or stupefy the brain. This was also proved by the fact that though the entire body may be paralysed, yet as long as the brain was uninjured the needle in the instrument would act as before. He also demonstrated that "subjects addicted to the habit of having recourse to drugs known as neuro-muscular agents," depressers of the reflex action of the spinal cord, such as chloral, chloroform, bromide of potassium, etc., were the less apt to produce (by looking at the instrument) a deflection or a succession of them in the registering needle; thus demonstrating that the transmission of cerebral force by external radiation was interfered with by the use of such drugs; the absence of the radiation produced by thought-force seeming to point out that the production of thought and the intensity of it was impaired by the ingestion and assimilation of those agents. Not only was such an effect produced by toxic drugs, but also by any kind of intoxication; i.e., by an excess of stimulants, whether in the form of drink or of food. Thus was the stupefying effect of drunkenness and voracity scientifically proved by this registering apparatus.

The same diminution of deflective power in a subject over the needle was caused by anger, violence (after the fit), and by envy, jealousy, hatred (during the fit). A subject being tested in the vicinity of a person he disliked or hated was shown by the instrument to *lose standard*; if in the vicinity of a person he liked or loved the standard denoted by the needle *was raised*.

He also demonstrated that an idiot had no power to deflect the needle in the apparatus, whereas a single look from a person endowed with brain-power might cause movements and deflections at distances varying from two to twenty feet.

Among the many interesting experiments made from time to time by the inventor and myself, was one described in a magazine article entitled "The Most Wonderful Machine in the World." It was to the effect that upon one occasion a gentleman stood in front of the instrument criticizing its action and endeavouring to find some explanation of its power. About the same time several other persons entered the room, and in casual conversation one of them mentioned the fact of a sudden fall in the value of a South African company's shares. No one knew that the gentleman looking at the machine was the holder of many thousands of pounds' worth of these shares; but at the moment the drop in the value was mentioned the man's mental emotion caused the indicator in the machine to move rapidly and register one of the highest numbers that has been recorded by it.

Another curious experiment was that in which one could determine which of two people loved more than the other. In this case the two persons were tested separately, and charts made of their movements shown by the machine. They were then left together for half an hour before being tested again. The one whose love was strongest was found to have a greater influence on the instrument, while the other was found to have lost power over the registering needle, in a greater or lesser degree, according to the effect produced by the other person's presence.

One of the most extraordinary conditions of the machine was that there was *no physical contact whatever required*. In the regular course of experiments the person to be tested stood within a foot to two feet of the instrument; but if the atmosphere was clear and dry, a person of a strong will might influence the needle at a distance of from ten to twenty feet.

No magnets were employed by the operator, nor was there any electric contact with the needle, except the unknown agent —be it odic force, magnetism, or something still more subtle that radiated from the brain through the body, and through the atmosphere to the machine. People tested this for themselves in every conceivable manner. The great unbelievers tried in every way to prove that the needle was moved by some other agency, but one and all in the end admitted that the action of the needle was due to a force given off by the person tested.

One of the leading divines in the Church of England, after seeing the machine being tested in a variety of ways, said: "Such a machine not only would convince one of the influence of mind over matter, but more importantly the influence of mind over mind; for if the radiation of our thoughts affect this needle of metal, how much more so must we not affect the thoughts, ideas, and lives of those around us."

In conclusion, may not then the very force that moved this needle be the very power that in its continual action marks the hand through the peripheral nerves. We know not, and may never know, why this unseen force should write the deeds of the past or the dreams of the future. And yet the prisoner in his dungeon will often write on the stones around him his name and legend, to be read or not, as the case may be. May not, then, the soul, as a captive in the body, write on the fleshly walls of its prison-house its past trials, its future hopes, the deeds that it will some day realize? For if there be a soul, then is it, being a spirit, conscious of all things, its past joys, its present sorrows, and the future—be it what it may.

PART V

CHAPTER 1

SOME INTERESTING HANDS

THE HAND OF H.H. THE INFANTA EULALIA

THE hand of H.H. the Infanta Eulalia of Spain shown on Plate II, is remarkable, if only for the quantity of lines that appear, most of them contradictory in their meanings, as was the character of the lady, the subject of this sketch.

The Infanta Eulalia was a clever, brilliant woman who could do almost anything and yet did nothing exceptionally well.

As Aunt to Alfonso XIII, ex-King of Spain, she had an exalted position in one of the most distinguished Courts of Europe. She, however, threw overboard her great opportunities, brought discredit on her position by her numerous adventures, made a failure of her marriage and lost the greater part of her fortune.

She could paint extremely well, had considerable talent as a writer and musician, could use a rifle and ride to hounds as few women can and yet for all practical purposes accomplished nothing very remarkable.

I reproduce this hand as an example of the line of Sun, that although appearing well in its early part, at about the middle of the palm crosses over and *finishes on the Mount of Saturn*, an extremely unfavourable indication on any hand, especially so if the line of fate appears to split up or lose its strength before it reaches its termination.

Other points for the student to notice are the downward curve of one end of the line of heart at its commencement under the Mount of Jupiter, the general appearance of the heart-line itself, the broken-up irregular Girdle of Venus, the drooping lines of marriage on the base of the fourth finger. The peculiarly marked line of head with an "island" in the centre, with one end terminating in a "star" on the second Mount of Mars, the indication of mental brilliancy, but of an erratic kind.

The Infanta Eulalia had an extraordinary magnetic personality, she was a delightful hostess, could speak fluently every European language, she attracted people to her and yet made innumerable enemies. (See lines crossing from Mount of Mars under Jupiter.)

In studying this hand, it is well to bear in mind that a vast number of lines have a tendency to contradict or *neutralize their meaning*. As a rule, it will be found that persons are more successful when the principal lines are clear and distinct and as it were, not confused by a multitude of minor marks running through them.

THE HAND OF GENERAL SIR REDVERS BULLER, V.C.

The right hand of General Sir Redvers Buller, Plate III, is a remarkable example of two lines of head on the same hand.

One is contained in the level line of head and heart crossing the palm from side to side. The other, the line from high up on Jupiter.

The lines from the line of life on the base of the first finger are also worthy of interest.

The hand itself is long, of the intellectual type, while the thumb stands out clear and distinct, the embodiment of will-power and determination.

The fourth or "little finger" is the one badly developed part of this hand, but Sir Redvers Buller was a man with no great command of language or gift of eloquence, and was unable to defend himself when the moment came when speech would have been a valuable asset. I have written about the indications given by the fourth finger in Chapter XI, Part I.

The lines of fate and Sun are also good up to the point where a line may be noticed crossing the line of Sun *toward* Saturn. This is not a good sign on any hand, as it indicates some reverse of fate, at about the time when this mark crosses the line of Sun.

General Sir Redvers Buller had extraordinary power and command over his men when he employed the gift of organization and authority conferred on him by the line of head coming from Jupiter.

There is, however, something contradictory and even un-lucky about persons who have the lines of head and heart running together across the palm. Such people have a kind of "single track" brain that will not listen to others or take any advice unless it comes from themselves. They may meet with con-siderable success due to their excessive power of concentration on some one object, until any mark on their line of Sun *bends or inclines toward the Mount of Saturn*. If such is the case their plans as suddenly turn out wrong and they usually meet with disaster.

Sir Redvers Buller was sceptical when I told him that there lay before him another campaign which would bring censure and criticism on him.

This actually occurred when, as Commander-in-Chief in the Boer War, the disaster of "Spion Kop" and the Modder River brought about his recall and censure by the War Office.

THE HAND OF SIR ARTHUR SULLIVAN, BART.

Sir Arthur Sullivan will be remembered for the original and beautiful music he composed for the "Gilbert and Sullivan Operas." The reproduction of his right hand on Plate IV, shows the line of head separated from that of the life, long and gently curved into the middle of the Mount of Luna. The space between the head- and life-lines denotes the dramatic quality of his work, while the curved line of head into the Mount of Luna indicates his great powers of imagination and originality.

The line of fate so closely tied to the Mount of Venus accurately portrays the difficulties of his early life when he sacrificed himself to help his family and relations. The second or inner fate-line starting out towards the middle of the line of life and rising upward into the Mount of Jupiter, in itself, promised successful ambition to be followed as it was later by the main line of fate also curving towards the same mount.

In spite of the recognition of his work by the public, hardly any lines of Sun can be seen on this hand, but it has to be remembered that this great composer had not by nature a sunny, happy disposition. He cared little or nothing for personal fame or glory, nor did his work bring him any great amount of worldly possession or wealth.

THE HAND OF WILLIAM WHITELEY

The hand of William Whiteley, Plate V, one of England's great business men, called "the Universal Provider" because his store was said to be able to supply anything from a "needle to a battleship," is a good example of "the business hand."

It is the square type with fairly long fingers and a very "level-headed" looking head-line, closely joined to the line of life. There was nothing rash or impulsive in William Whiteley's "make-up"; he was noted for his caution, but at the same time he was always ready for any emergency.

The fate-and Sun-lines on this hand are well marked. There is one peculiar line rising from the centre of the line of fate toward the base of the Mount of Jupiter, but which appears to be cut through by a line from Mars to the Sun. This occurs at the age he had reached when he was shot and killed in his office by his supposed illegitimate son.

When I took the impression of his hand I warned him of danger of a violent death.

Very calmly he asked: "How far off is that danger?"

I replied: "About thirteen years from now."

Then thirteen years later he was shot to death at the height of his enormously successful business career.

THE HAND OF THE RIGHT HON. JOSEPH CHAMBERLAIN, M.P., AND HIS SON, WHO LATER BECAME SIR AUSTEN CHAMBERLAIN

These two right hands, Plates VI and VII, are good examples of heredity as shown by hands. It will be noticed that the shape is similar in both father and son, while the lines are very much alike.

I took these impressions in Mr. Chamberlain's private room in the House of Commons. Mr. Chamberlain was keenly interested in my predictions that his son Austen was destined to follow the same political career that he had done.

It is common knowledge that as the years went past, Austen Chamberlain filled one by one the exalted positions his father had occupied in Government life. He entered Parliament at the same age, and successively filled the positions of Postmaster General, Chancellor of the Exchequer, Leader of the House of Commons and finally received knighthood for his services as President of the Locarno Peace Conference after the war.

Further, he suffered the same class of illness which his distinguished father passed through and at the same periods of his life, even to the serious nervous breakdown that caused him to retire from public life (see health-line attacking the line of life) which caused paralysis to his father in his sixty-third and sixty-fifth year.

CHEIRO'S OWN HAND

In Plate VIII, I reproduce an impression of my own hand as an example of what is called "the double line of head."

I have stated in previous pages of this book (Chapter VII), that "a double line of head" is very rarely found. The character shown by each of these lines of head is in apparent contradiction to the other. For example, the lower line closely joined to the line of life denotes a mentality extremely sensitive, artistic and imaginative.

The upper line gives the reverse characteristics: namely, rising on the Mount of Jupiter and running nearly straight across the palm, it denotes self-confidence, ambition, power to dominate others and a level-headed, practical way of looking at life.

One can hardly imagine such mentally opposite characteristics in the same person, but the impression given of my own hand is a good illustration of these statements.

On my left hand there is no sign whatever of any upper head-line—there is only the lower line to be seen; and it is a curious fact that the appearance of the upper head-line on my right hand only commenced to be noticeable when I was about thirty years of age.

At this period of my life, circumstances brought me before the world as a lecturer and public speaker. This forced me to make a supreme effort to overcome my extreme sensitiveness as shown by the lower head-line, with the result that the upper line began to develop and in a few years became *the dominant one* on my right hand.

I have also stated that in cases where "the double line of head" is found, persons who possess these lines are inclined to live what are called "double lives" of one form or another.

In my own particular case this has been remarkably true, for more than thirty years one section of the public only knew me under my *nom de guerre* as "Cheiro," while another section only knew me under my own name.

I can further state here, that due to the influence of the more sensitive side of my nature, for many years I gave vent to my feelings by writing poetry, both sentimental and religious, while at the same time, the other side was engaged in appearing as a lecturer on the public platform, as War Correspondent, and later, as editor of newspapers in London and Paris.

These "double lines" of head may be very clearly seen in the impression of my right hand reproduced in this volume.

A BABY'S HAND TWENTY-FOUR HOURS OLD

The impression of this baby's right hand I took twenty-four hours after its birth. Impressions of very young children's hands are very hard to take, as the flesh is so soft and pliable and the little ones will not keep still.

In this case, Plate IX, I succeeded very well and the lines may be quite clearly seen. I made this impression many years ago and the "baby" has now grown to be a man. He has done very well in a business career (probably due to the upper line of head lying so straight across the hand).

THE HAND OF MADAME SARAH BERNHARDT

The most remarkable point about this imprint (Plate X) is, the lines of fate and Sun rising so early in life from almost the wrist and running *parallel to one another to the advanced years of the life.*

The "great Sarah" commenced her dramatic career at the age of sixteen. In spite of her remarkable talents she had many difficulties to contend with, up to the period when on her hand the two lines of fate may be seen coming together about her twenty-sixth year. From this date on her fame and renown became world-wide.

The line of head is clear as if drawn by a rule, while the open space between it and the line of life denotes her impulsiveness and dramatic ability which I called attention to in Chapter VII of Part II.

It will be noticed the remarkable number of small lines that appear to be shot out of the line of life in an upward direction. These indicate what may be termed "spurts of energy" at these moments.

These are not good signs, if a heavily-marked line of health is seen attacking the life-line from the Mount of Mercury. In Madame Bernhardt's case there is hardly any health-line, it appears to stop, or fade out, after her early years. As is well known, the great actress had a wonderfully strong constitution once she passed her middle years, which continued to the last period of her life.

Madame Bernhardt was born in Paris, October 22, 1845. She died in Paris, March 26, 1923, in her seventy-eighth year.

THE RIGHT HAND OF DAME MELBA, G.B.E., THE FAMOUS AUSTRALIAN PRIMA DONNA

It will be noticed that the line of head (Plate XI) is separated by a space between it and the line of life, very much alike to that on Sarah Bernhardt's hand, it also rises on the base of the Mount of Jupiter giving the qualities of great ambition.

In Chapter V of Part II in dealing with the line of life I wrote: "When there is a medium space between the line of life and that of head, the subject is more free to carry out his or her plans and ideas; it also denotes energy and a very go-ahead spirit." In speaking of the line of head in Chapter VII, I said: "When a space is found between the line of head and that of life, it is beneficial when not too wide; when medium it denotes splendid energy and self-confidence and is a useful sign for barristers, actors, preachers, etc."

Dame Melba had all those qualities that suited her for a life before the public. Both the fate- and Sun-lines on her hand are also sharply marked, especially the line of Sun culminating, as it does, in the form of a triangle at the base of the mount of that name.

In estimating the ultimate success of a person's life, it is always wise to notice if these lines of fate and Sun *appear equal to one another.*

The "double life-line" that may be noticed about the middle of the hand gave Dame Melba enormous vitality and by running outward into a line of travel towards Luna, promised the almost continual run of long voyages from one side of the world to the other which was so much a part of this remarkable woman's career.

Dame Melba consulted me in New York when she wrote in my Visitor's Book:

"'Cheiro' you are *wonderful*—what more can I say?"

"NELLIE MELBA."

THE HAND OF LORD LEIGHTON, P.R.A.

Sir Frederick Leighton, who later became Lord Leighton, had just been elected President of the Royal Academy when he gave me the impression of his hand which appears on Plate XII. His left and right were exactly alike; for some reason of his own he preferred that in my book I should reproduce the left.

For a man's hand, it is almost a perfect example of the "Conic or Artistic" type, which I have described in Chapter VI, Part I, but in Lord Leighton's case, his hands were strong and elastic, which gave him the strength of will to hold in check his natural love of luxury and comfort. His artistic disposition, characteristic of this type, was, however, much in evidence in his beautiful studio and in his home, where he lived more like a Persian prince in a palace than an Englishman.

The line of Sun from the wrist to the third finger is very remarkable. It promised him the fame and glory which came easily to him from the very commencement of his brilliant career.

Lord Leighton studied hands from the standpoint of his art and in all his pictures emphasized their shape and expression.

THE HAND OF "MARK TWAIN"

The right hand of "Mark Twain," Plate XIII, does not come out as clear as one would like. It was made by means of smoked paper, a process I employed in the earlier days of my career. I later substituted a process I will describe later on in these pages.

The most remarkable thing to notice in the impression of the right hand of this celebrated American humorist is that the line of head lies almost *level across the palm*. This characteristic is found on the hands of persons who develop the faculty of "seeing both sides" of anything that interests them.

"Mark Twain" had this particular gift in a very marked way and which comes out strongly in all his writings. He was not a "visionary" by any manner of means. If anything he was an avowed sceptic and had to have facts to support his views or ideas.

When he came to see me I did not know who he was. While I was taking impressions of his hands, he said: "The past may leave its mark, I admit, and character may be told down to its finest shades of expression; all that I might believe—but how the future may be even foreshadowed is what I cannot understand."

In answer to his argument I took up the question of heredity. I showed him an impression of a mother's left and right hands with the imprints of five of her children's until we came to one where the right hand of the child tallied closely with the markings of the mother's right hand.

"In this case," I said, "which you can follow up and prove for yourself, every section of this girl's life repeated, even to dates, the events of the mother's life, although twenty years separated them in time.

"Now," I concluded, "if one had known the events of the mother's life and seen that the same markings appeared in the hands of the child—then, even say at six years of age, one could have predicted the events which would take place in the fate of the daughter."

This interested my visitor so deeply that he took notes of the various hands and was particularly struck by the fact that even the circles in the skin of the tops of the thumbs of the mother and this child agreed very closely.

As he was going he told me who he was and added: "The one humorous point in the situation is, that I came here expecting to lose my money by my foolishness, but I have gained a plot for a story which I certainly think should be a 'best seller.'"

A short time later he published *Pudd'n Head Wilson*, dealing with thumb-marks, which had an enormous success.

Before he left he wrote in my Visitor's Book the following:

"'Cheiro' has exposed my character to me with humiliating accuracy. I ought not to confess this accuracy, still I am moved to do it.

"MARK TWAIN."

THE HAND OF A CONVICTED MURDERER

I obtained the impression of Dr. Meyer's hand under the following conditions. On the occasion of my first visit to New York, some reporters representing the *New York World* called and said they wanted to test my powers by having me read imprints of hands without my knowing the names or positions of any of the people. Without demurring, I accepted the test and we at once got to work.

I had described the character and careers of perhaps a dozen of these test cases, when the impressions of a strange-looking pair of hands were put before me. I was struck by the fact that the lines on the left were in every way normal while those on the right were as abnormal as possible. I particularly noticed that on the left hand the line of head lay clear and straight across the centre, whereas on the right it appeared to have twisted out of its place, closing in against the heart-line under the base of the third finger.

I summed up the impressions before me by stating: " Judging from these hands, the owner of them undoubtedly commenced his career in a normal way. He is likely to have been a religious man in his early years." I thought that it was probable he might have commenced life as a Sunday-school teacher and later become interested in science or medicine.

I went on to describe how the man's entire nature slowly and steadily had changed under the continual urge to acquire wealth at any cost, until he was finally prepared even to commit murder for money.

My remarks noted down by the reporters were as follows: "Whether this man has committed one crime or twenty is not the question, as he enters his forty-fourth year he will be found out, arrested, tried and sentenced to death. It will then be proved, that for years he has used his mentality and whatever profession he has followed to obtain money by crime and has stopped at nothing to achieve his ends. This man in his forty-fourth year will pass through some sensational trial, he will be condemned to die, yet his hands show that he will escape this fate and live on for years—but in prison."

When the interview with me appeared the following Sunday in the *New York World*, the paper disclosed that the hands I had read were those of a Dr. Meyer from Chicago. He had that very week been arrested on suspicion of having poisoned wealthy patients whom he had insured for considerable amounts of money.

The trial, as might be expected, was a sensational one, but in spite of the efforts of the best lawyers, he was sentenced to die by the electric chair. The conviction was appealed against. Three trials in all took place, but at the third he was again condemned to death without hope of a reprieve.

A week before his execution, he requested that I should go and see him. I was taken to his cell in Sing Sing prison. As long as I live, I shall never forget the interview.

"Cheiro," gasped the now completely broken man, "at that interview you gave the reporters, what you said about my early life was true. But you also said that although I should be sentenced to the electric chair, I should live on for years—but in prison.

"I have lost my third and last appeal—in a few days I am to be executed. For God's sake, tell me if you stand by your words—that I shall escape 'the chair.'"

Even if I had not seen his line of life going on clear and distinct well past his forty-fourth year, I believe I would have tried to give him hope. To me it was torture to see that poor wretch before me, to feel his cold clammy hands touching mine, and see his hollow eyes hungry for a word of comfort.

Although I could hardly believe what I saw, I pointed out that his line of life showed no sign of any break, and so I left him, giving the hope that some miracle could still happen that would save him from the dreaded "chair."

Day after day went past, with no news to relieve the tension. Mentally I suffered almost as much as the poor man in the condemned cell. The evening papers, full of details of the preparations for the execution fixed for the next morning were eagerly bought up. I bought one and read every line.

Midnight came. Suddenly boys rushed through the streets

screaming "Special Edition." I read across the front page, "MEYER ESCAPES THE CHAIR, SUPREME COURT FINDS FLAW IN INDICTMENT." The miracle had happened. The sentence was altered to imprisonment for life. Meyer lived for fifteen years. When the end did come, he died peacefully in the prison hospital.

If students study this hand, they will see how closely its indications follow the descriptions I have given of the line of head showing the tendencies for premeditated murder in early pages of this book. Students must not confuse this rising line of head *against the heart-line* with the one straight line of head and heart combined, which will be seen in further impressions given later.

THE HAND OF A SUICIDE

Plate XV shows the hand of a woman who was possessed with suicidal mania. In this case the line of head may be seen sloping sharply downward toward the wrist under the Mount of Luna.

This young woman, although she had a good home, developed acute suicidal mania at the age of eighteen. She tried to kill herself on four different occasions until she finally succeeded in her purpose as she entered her twenty-eighth year. Note that her hand belongs to the long *narrow* psychic type with "philosophic" joints to the fingers, corresponding to my description of the Psychic Hand in Chapter VII, Part I.

It is interesting to bear in mind that this young girl had the Circle of Saturn at the base of the second finger with a line from it cutting the line of life at about her age of twenty-eight and on the line of Sun the commencement of an "island" at about the same date.

The line of head when sloping *under* the base of the Mount of Luna is a much more positive indication of acute suicidal mania than when the line of head curves downward into the face of the Mount of Luna. In the latter case the subject has a naturally despondent nature which only requires some added blow of fate or disappointment, which the highly imaginative disposition exaggerates (sloping head-line on Luna), to bring about the fatal act.

CHAPTER II

HOW TO MAKE CLEAR IMPRESSIONS OF HANDS

PRINTERS' ink, especially the kind employed by the police for fingerprints in all cities, is the best means I have found for making good impressions of hands.

Readers can purchase this ink at any establishment where they sell printers' materials.

At the same place, get a small gelatine roller, which is generally fitted in a metal frame with a wooden handle.

Next, get a few quires of *white coated paper* about the size of an ordinary sheet of typewriting paper. I specify *coated* or *glazed* paper, as it takes the best imprints. When you have obtained these requisites, go to any hardware store and get a rubber mat about a quarter to a half inch thick, what is called a "kneeling mat" will do very well. These are necessary to make a springy cushion, so that the fine lines come out clearly.

Place a sheet of the coated white paper on the upper surface of the rubber mat. Smooth out a small portion of the printers' ink by running the gelatine roller over it on a piece of glass.

When all is ready, run the gelatine roller over the subject's left and right hands, press them firmly down on the sheet of paper, turn the hand *over on the back* and with the flat part of the thumb press the paper lightly into the hollow of the palm and wrist, peel off the sheet of paper, starting from the fingers, and you will find you have obtained a clear impression of all the lines of the hand.

You may at first find some difficulty with persons who have a dry, acid skin, which may make the imprints in many cases look "spotted." This can be got over by first washing the hands you are going to treat with warm water, drying them thoroughly and sprinkling with a light dusting of some powder like talc. If you have not got talc, a little flour or chalk will do as well.

There are many ways of removing the printers' ink from the

hands.   The simplest and best is to get a small tin of the powder sold at all motor supply stores for cleaning oil and grease off hands, rub this on the hands in hot water and the ink will come off easily.

Alternatively, a few drops of petrol will do equally well, although it may not be quite so quick in its action.

Once the impressions are made on coated paper by printers' ink, they dry rapidly and will, for all practical purposes, last for ever.

I advise that the imprints should be signed and dated, so that they may always be identified.   I further suggest that the date and place of the subject's birth should be jotted down on the back of each impression, also that a drawing of one of the fingers should be included, showing the nail and noting down whether the "moons" are large or small.

An A.B.C. classeur of the kind used in offices for filing, will also be found useful in order to find rapidly any imprints which may have been stored away.

Another but more elaborate method of making very clear impressions is to soak a sheet of white paper in oil (in this case the paper need not be the coated or the glazed kind) press the hand with the printers' ink on it and finish as previously explained.

This method is useful in cases where the skin of the hand is very dry or difficult to take on account of marked acidity.

INDEX